POWERPOINT 2002

in easy steps

STEPHEN COPESTAKE

In easy steps is an imprint of Computer Step
Southfield Road . Southam
Warwickshire CV47 0FB . England

http://www.ineasysteps.com

Notice of Liability
Every effort has been made to ensure that this book contains accurate
and current information. However, Computer Step and the author
shall not be liable for any loss or damage suffered by readers as a
result of any information contained herein.

Trademarks
Microsoft® and Windows® are registered trademarks of Microsoft
Corporation. All other trademarks are acknowledged as belonging to
their respective companies.

Printed and bound in the United Kingdom

ISBN 1-84078-145-9

Table of Contents

Slide design   69

Working with objects   87

Using charts   103

Using multimedia 121

6

Using speech recognition 141

7

Finalising slide shows 145

8

Preparing slide shows

Presenting slide shows

Index

First steps

Here, you'll get started quickly with PowerPoint 2002. You'll specify which toolbars display; use Ask-a-Question and online HELP; work with views; and set Zoom levels. You'll also undo/redo errors and use advanced features (these include Quick File Switching; error repair; copying/pasting multiple items; using the Task Pane/Smart Tags; and signing slide shows digitally).

Covers

Chapter One

The PowerPoint 2002 screen

When you've instructed PowerPoint 2002 to create a new presentation based on a template or with the help of the AutoContent Wizard (see chapter 2), or if you've elected to open an existing presentation, the final result will look something like this:

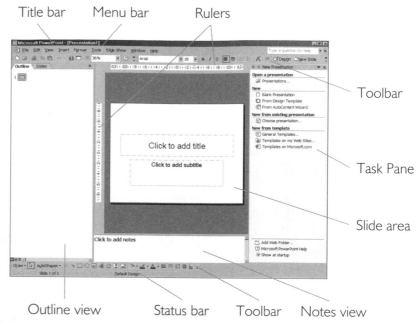

Title bar   Menu bar   Rulers

Toolbar

Task Pane

Slide area

Outline view   Status bar   Toolbar   Notes view

Where Outline view is currently displayed you can also display Thumbnail view – see pages 15–16.

Note, however, that this is simply one 'view': Normal view. PowerPoint 2002 lets you interact with presentations in various ways. It does this by providing the following additional major views:

• Outline

• Slide Sorter

• Notes Page

See pages 15–17 later for more information.

Working with toolbars

Toolbars are collections of icons. By clicking on the appropriate icon, you can launch a specific PowerPoint 2002 feature. Using toolbars saves you having to pull down menus and use dialogs.

PowerPoint 2002 comes with some 13 toolbars. Some of the most frequently used are:

The Task Pane is classed as a toolbar – for more on using the Task Pane, see page 26.

Standard	The most useful toolbar. Use this to open and save presentations, and to perform copy/cut and paste operations. Also used to:

— launch HELP

— insert new slides

— print presentations

— change the slide Zoom (magnification) level

— insert charts

— undo or redo editing actions

— launch Print Preview to preview your slides before printing

Formatting	Use this to apply formatting options to slides and text
Drawing	Use this to create shapes and lines, and to customise shape and line colour/formatting
Picture	Use this to insert disk-based pictures into slides, and to format them
Web	Use this to go to World Wide Web sites instantly (providing you have a live Internet connection), and to navigate through web pages once you've arrived
Outlining	Use this to work with Outline view (for example, you can use the Outlining toolbar to hide or reveal slide levels)

See chapter 2 for more on working with slide outlines.

Specifying which toolbars display

You can have as many toolbars on-screen as you need.

Pull down the View menu and carry out the following steps:

You can also activate a toolbar by right-clicking an existing one and ticking its entry in the shortcut menu.

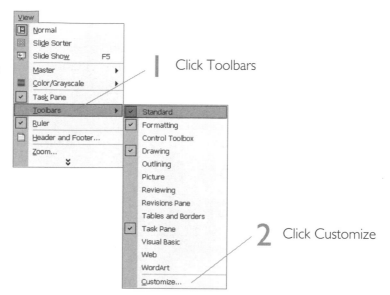

Click Toolbars

2 Click Customize

To add a new button to a toolbar, click the Commands tab instead. In the Categories field, click a category (a group of associated icons). In the Commands box, drag a button onto the toolbar in the open presentation. Finally, click Close.

(To delete a toolbar button, select the Commands tab then drag the relevant icon off the toolbar. Finally, click Close.)

3 Ensure the Toolbars tab is active

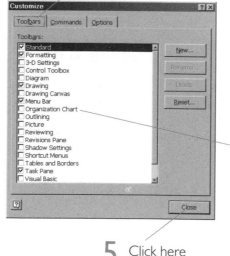

4 Tick or untick one or more toolbar entries to display or hide them respectively

5 Click here

Automatic customisation

As you use PowerPoint, individual features are dynamically promoted or demoted in the relevant menus.
This means menus are continually evolving...

Until PowerPoint 2000, it was true that, although different users use different features, no allowance had been made for this: the same features displayed on everyone's menus and toolbars...

Now, however, menus and toolbars are personalised in PowerPoint 2002.

Personalised menus

When you first run PowerPoint, its menus display the features which Microsoft believes are used 95% of the time. Features which are infrequently used are not immediately visible. This is made clear in the illustrations below:

PowerPoint menus expand automatically. Simply pull down the required menu, (which will at first be abbreviated) then wait a few seconds: it expands to display the full menu.
However, to expand a menu manually, click here on the chevrons at the bottom:

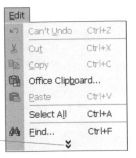

The Edit menu,

as it first

appears...

Automatic customisation also applies to toolbars. Note the following:

- *if possible, they display on a single row*
- *they overlap when there isn't enough room on-screen*
- *icons are 'promoted' and 'demoted' like menu entries*
- *demoted icons are shown in a separate fly-out, reached by clicking:*

...the expanded

menu

Ask-a-Question

In PowerPoint 2000, users had to run the Office Assistant (see the tip) to get answers to plain-English questions. In PowerPoint 2002, however, this isn't the case. Simply do the following:

The Office Assistant is turned off by default. To turn it on, pull down the Help menu and click Show Office Assistant.

The Assistant is an animated (and frequently unpopular) helper which answers questions, but you can achieve the same effect more easily with Ask-a-Question.

Type in your question here and press Enter

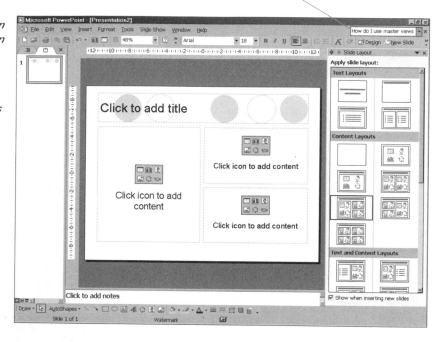

Re step 2 – if there are more topics to be viewed, click See More instead to access them.

- Troubleshoot PowerPoint views
- Replace or add slide masters
- About the title master
- None of the above, search for more on the Web

2 Click a relevant entry

3 Optional – click Show All to display all sub-topics

Use the Contents and Index tabs as you would in any other program.

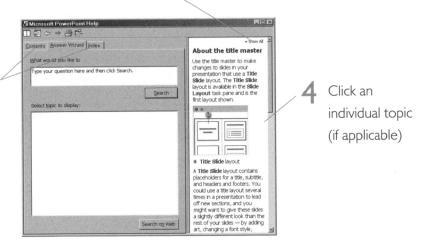

4 Click an individual topic (if applicable)

The result of step 3 – all the topics are enlarged (the expanded text is shown in green)

To print out a topic, click this icon:

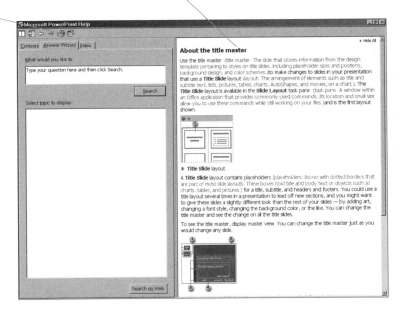

Undo and Redo

To set the number of undo levels, pull down the Tools menu and select Options. In the Options dialog, select the Edit tab. In the Maximum number of undos field, insert a new limit (the default is 20, the maximum 150).

PowerPoint lets you reverse – 'undo' – most editing operations (exceptions are Zoom operations and file saves). If, subsequently, you decide that you do want to proceed with an operation that you've reversed, you can 'redo' it.

You can even undo or redo a series of operations in one go.

You can undo and redo actions in the following ways (in descending order of complexity):

- via the keyboard

- from within the Edit menu

- from within the Standard toolbar

If you haven't used the Undo or Redo buttons recently, they may be in the flyout. To access this, click this button on the right of the toolbar:

Using the keyboard
Simply press Ctrl+Z to undo an action, or Ctrl+Y to reinstate it.

Using the Edit menu
Pull down the Edit menu and click Undo… or Redo… as appropriate (the ellipses denote the precise nature of the action to be reversed or reinstated).

Using the Standard toolbar
Carry out the following action to undo an action (see the DON'T FORGET tip for how to reinstate it):

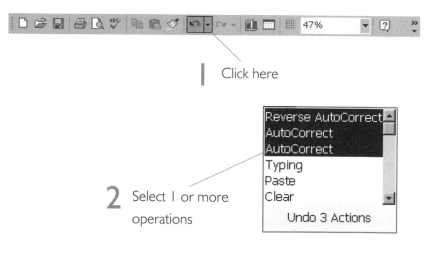

Click here

To redo an action (i.e. reverse an undo), do the following in the Standard toolbar:

Click here

In the list, select one or more redos (note the tip below also applies).

2 Select 1 or more operations

Re step 2 – if you select an early operation in the list (i.e. one near the bottom), all later operations are included.

The slide views – an overview

Note that Normal view includes the following additional features:

- *Outline view – shows the textual structure underlying slides*
- *Thumbnail view – shows each slide as a thumbnail (as in Slide Sorter view)*
- *Notes view – shows the speaker notes associated with the active slide*

PowerPoint has the following views:

Normal   displays each slide individually

Slide Sorter shows all the slides as icons, so you can manipulate them more easily

Notes Page   shows each slide together with any speaker notes

These are different ways of looking at your slide show. Normal view provides a very useful overview, while Slide Sorter view lets you modify more than one slide at a time.

Switching to a view

Pull down the View menu and do the following:

Normal view is also known as Tri-Pane view.

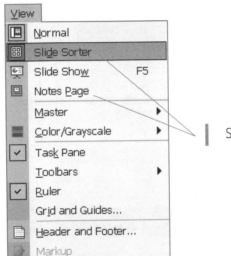

Select a view

There are also various Master views – see chapter 3 for how to use these.

These views are also discussed in later chapters.

Using the slide views

You can use Thumbnail view to perform operations which are available in Slide Sorter view. Right-click any slide icon and select the relevant operation from the menu:

The following are some brief supplemental notes on how best to use the PowerPoint 2002 views.

Normal view

Normal view displays the current slide in its own window. Use Normal view when you want a detailed picture of a slide (for instance, when you amend any of the slide contents, or when you change the overall formatting).

Select a tab here to view slides in Outline view (you can amend this and watch your changes take effect in the Slide area on the right) or in Thumbnail view (as here)

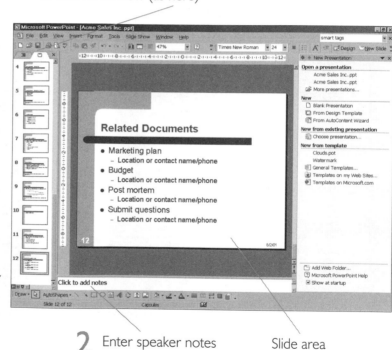

To jump to the next or earlier slide, press Page Down or Page Up respectively.

Resize Thumbnail view via its splitter bar:

Drag here

2 Enter speaker notes   Slide area

Slide Sorter view

If you need to rearrange the order of slides, use Slide Sorter view. You can simply click on a slide and drag it to a new location (to move more than one slide, hold down one Ctrl key as you click them, then release the key and drag). You can also copy a slide by holding down Ctrl *as you drag*.

You can also use Slide Sorter view to apply a new slide layout to more than one slide at a time – see chapter 2.

Slide Sorter view gives you a useful overview – use it near the end of the slide show creation process to verify everything is as you want it.

In Normal and Notes Page views, you can also use the vertical scroll bar to move to specific slides.

As you drag the scroll bar, PowerPoint 2002 displays a message telling you the number and title of the slide you're up to:.

Slide: 1 of 2
[Company Name] Certificat…

To specify a default view, choose Tools, Options. Complete the Default view section.

Re step 1 on the right – you can also do this in Normal view. Follow step 2 on the facing page.

To perform additional operations, right-click any slide and select an entry in the shortcut menu

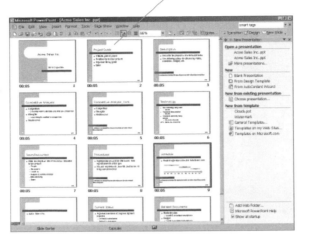

Slide Sorter view

Notes Page view

This view is an aid to the presenter rather than the viewer of the slide show. If you want to enter speaker notes on a slide (for later printing), use Notes Page view.

The slide is displayed at a reduced size

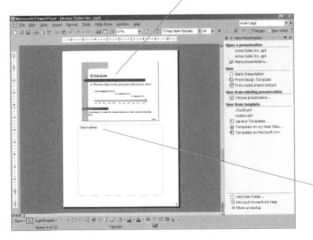

Enter notes (see chapter 8 for how to do this)

Using Zoom

You can also use the Zoom button to set Zoom levels. In the Standard toolbar, do the following:.

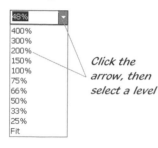

Click the arrow, then select a level

It's often useful to be able to inspect your presentations in close up; this is called 'zooming in'. Alternatively, sometimes taking an overview ('zooming out') is beneficial.

You can zoom in and out in any PowerPoint 2002 view (although the available options vary).

Setting the Zoom level

Pull down the View menu and do the following:

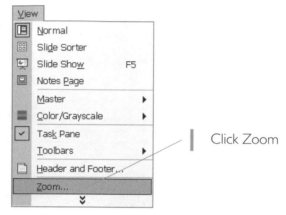

Click Zoom

Re the above tip – if you haven't used it for some time, the Zoom button may be on the Standard toolbar fly-out instead.

If you want to use your own Zoom level (rather than a set figure), type in the zoom % here:
(The maximum zoom setting in Normal and Notes Page views is 400%; the lowest is 10%. The maximum in Slide Sorter view is 100% and the lowest 20%.)
Finally, carry out step 3.

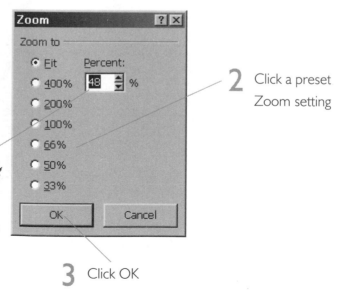

2 Click a preset Zoom setting

3 Click OK

Using HELP

PowerPoint calls these highly specific HELP bubbles 'ToolTips'.

ToolTips are a specialised form of ScreenTips (see below).

PowerPoint supports the standard Windows HELP system. For instance:

- Moving the mouse pointer over toolbar buttons produces an explanatory HELP bubble:

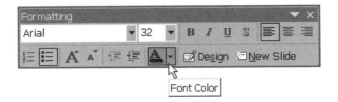

- You can move the mouse pointer over fields in dialogs, commands or screen areas and produce a specific HELP box. Carry out the following procedure to achieve this:

PowerPoint calls these highly specific HELP topics 'ScreenTips'.

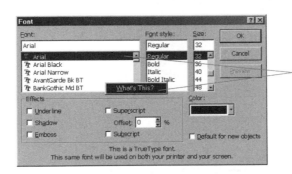

Right-clicking a field and left-clicking the box which launches...

Click the font you want to apply to the selected text. TrueType fonts and printer fonts are designated by icons. Fonts with no icon next to them are native Windows fonts.

...produces a specific HELP topic

Other standard Windows HELP features are also present; see your Windows documentation for how to use these.

Install on Demand

PowerPoint 2002 makes use of a feature which allows users to install program components on demand, only when they're needed. Uninstalled components still have the following triggers:

- shortcuts

- icons

- menu entries

within PowerPoint 2002.

On your system, Pack and Go may already have been fully installed.

An example of Install on Demand is Pack and Go (a special program component used to 'package' slide shows so that they can be run on computers on which PowerPoint is not installed):

1 Pull down the File menu and do the following:

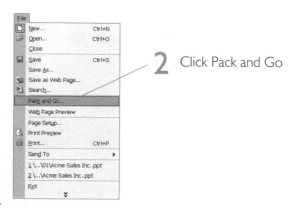

2 Click Pack and Go

The Pack and Go wizard compresses your presentation – for fuller information on the wizard, see pages 181–182.

3 Complete the wizard which launches. When you click Finish in the final screen, the following message launches:

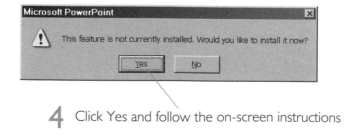

4 Click Yes and follow the on-screen instructions

Collect and Paste

You can copy multiple items to the Office Clipboard from within any Windows program which supports copy-and-paste, but you can only paste in the last one (except in PowerPoint or other Office modules).

Using PowerPoint 2002, if you want to copy-and-paste multiple items of text and/or pictures into a presentation, you can now copy as many as 24 items. These are stored in a special version of the Windows Clipboard called the Office Clipboard, which in turn is located in the Task Pane. The Office Clipboard displays a visual representation of the data.

Using the Office Clipboard

Use standard procedures to copy multiple examples of text and/or pictures – after the first copy, the Clipboard appears in the Task Pane. Do the following:

To clear the contents of the Office Clipboard, click Clear All.

To call up the Office Clipboard at any time, pull down the Edit menu and click Office Clipboard.

Copying items bigger than 4Mb (with up to 64Mb of RAM) or 8Mb (with more than 64Mb) to the Office Clipboard will mean it can accept no further data.

Click the data you want to insert – it appears at the insertion point

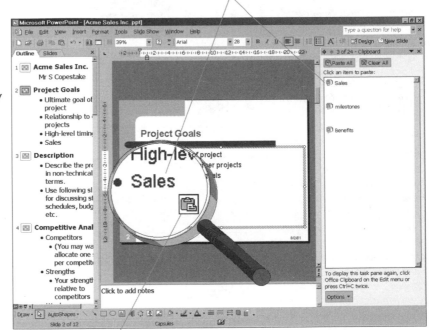

2 A Smart Tag may appear – see overleaf

Using Smart Tags

Re step 2 – choose Keep Source Formatting to retain the pasted text's original format, or Use Design Template Formatting (self-explanatory).

PowerPoint recognises certain types of data and underlines them with a dotted purple underline or a small blue box. When you move the mouse pointer over the line/box an 'action button' appears with access to commands which would otherwise have to be accessed from menus/toolbars or other programs.

The Paste Options button

Note that Smart Tags also appear when you do the following:

- *resize text automatically with AutoFit*

- *insert pictures, diagrams etc. which change the slide layout*

1 Text has been copied and pasted in...

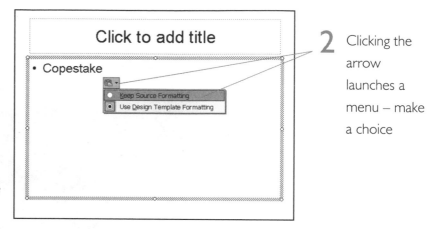

2 Clicking the arrow launches a menu – make a choice

Here, you can opt to have the AutoCorrect correction undone just this once ('Undo Automatic Corrections') or you can stop the correction being made in future ('Stop Automatically Correcting "abbout"').
(In this instance, you can also select 'Stop Auto-capitalizing First Letter of Sentences' to have PowerPoint refrain from applying capitals to the start of sentences.)

The AutoCorrect button

1 An AutoCorrect entry replaces 'abbout' with 'about'

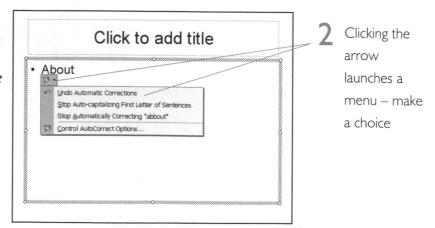

2 Clicking the arrow launches a menu – make a choice

See chapter 2 for more on using AutoCorrect.

Quick File Switching

In order to use Quick File Switching you need to be using:

- *Windows 98/2000/Me/ XP, or:*

- *Windows 95 with Internet Explorer 4.0 (or a later version)*

In the past, only programs (not individual windows within programs) displayed on the Windows Taskbar. With PowerPoint 2002, however, all open windows display as separate buttons.

In the following example, three presentations have been loaded. All three display as separate windows, although only one copy of PowerPoint 2002 is running:

Three PowerPoint 2002 windows

This is clarified by a glance at the Window menu which (as before) shows all open windows:

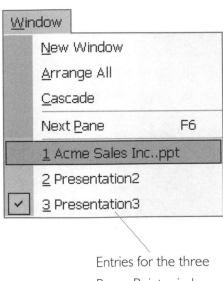

Entries for the three
PowerPoint windows

Use this technique to go to a presentation window by simply clicking its Taskbar button, a considerable saving in time and effort.

Repairing errors

PowerPoint 2002 provides a special feature you can use to repair damage to modules.

Detect and Repair

Do the following to correct program errors (but note selecting Discard my customised settings and restore default settings in step 3 will ensure that all default settings are restored, so any you've customised – including menu/toolbar positions and view settings – will be lost):

1 Pull down the Help menu and do the following:

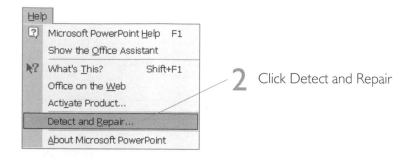

2 Click Detect and Repair

3 Select one or both options

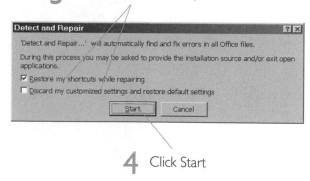

4 Click Start

5 Follow the on-screen instructions – Detect and Repair can be a lengthy process

6 You may have to re-enter your user name and initials when you restart PowerPoint

You can also use a further procedure for instances when PowerPoint hangs (ceases to respond).

Application Recovery

When errors occur, PowerPoint should give you the option of saving open files before the application closes.

1 Click Start, Programs, Microsoft Office Tools, Microsoft Office Application Recovery

2 Select Microsoft PowerPoint, or the presentation which isn't responding

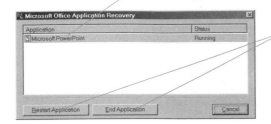

3 Click Recover Application to try to recover the slide show(s) you were working on, or End Application to close PowerPoint with data loss

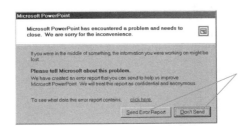

4 Select Send Error Report to email error details to Microsoft, or Don't Send

This is the Document Recovery Task Pane: When you've finished with it, click Close.

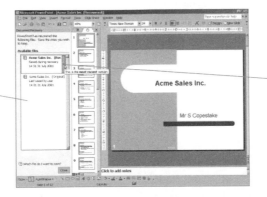

5 (If necessary) open PowerPoint. Click the slide show you want to keep (usually the most recent). In the menu, select Open or View to view it or Save As to save it

The PowerPoint Task Pane

The use of the Task Pane is also covered at appropriate locations throughout this book.

PowerPoint 2002 provides a special pane on the right of the screen which you can use to launch various tasks. The main incarnations of the Task Pane are:

- New Presentation

- Clipboard

- Search

- Insert Clip Art

Using the Task Pane

To display or hide the Task Pane, pull down the View menu and click Task Pane.

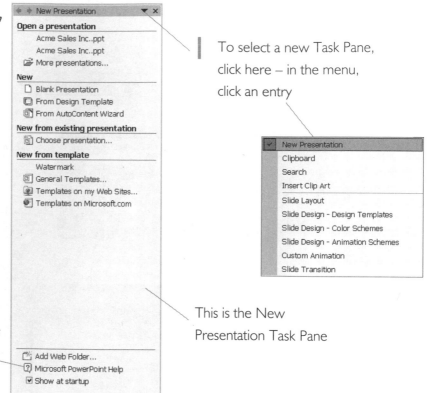

To select a new Task Pane, click here – in the menu, click an entry

This is the New Presentation Task Pane

In the New Presentation Task Pane, click here:
to launch

HELP.

Digital signatures

You can attach digital signatures to PowerPoint presentations, as a way of enhancing security. The signature confirms that the presentation was sent by you and hasn't been altered in any way, and uses a digital certificate.

Creating digital certificates

If you can't find SELFCERT.EXE, go to Control Panel. Click the entry for Office XP and select Add/Remove. Opt to amend the existing installation then double-click Office Shared Features. Enable Digital Signature for VBA Projects.

Running the procedure here creates a self-certification. Self-certification doesn't carry the weight of certification by a formal certification authority (see overleaf).

1 Locate a file called SELFCERT.EXE (usually in the C:\Program Files\Microsoft Office\Office 10\ folder)

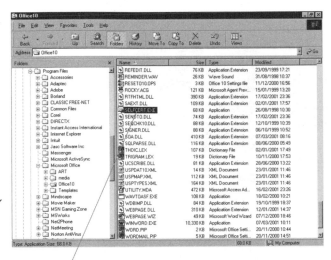

2 Double-click SELFCERT.EXE

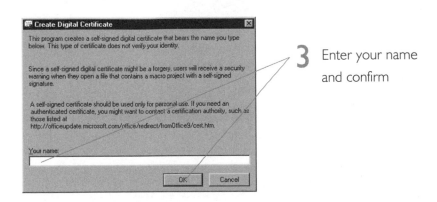

3 Enter your name and confirm

Applying digital signatures

If you're using PowerPoint as a member of an organisation, it may have its own certification authority. Contact your network administrator or IT department for more information.

1 Pull down the Tools menu and click Options.

2 Click the Security tab

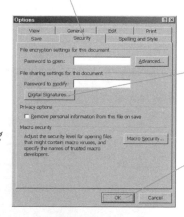

Digitally signing presentations may have no legal validity.

3 Click Digital Signatures

7 Click OK

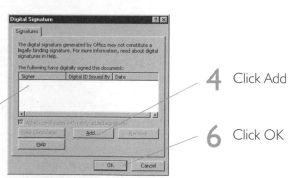

To remove a digital signature, select it here and click Remove.

4 Click Add

6 Click OK

You can only apply signatures to presentations which have been saved (PowerPoint reminds you if this isn't the case).

By the same token, saving a presentation after you've signed it removes the signature.

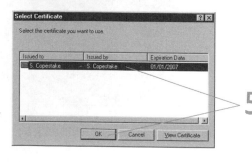

5 Select a certificate and confirm

Saving configuration settings

You can use a special wizard – the Save My Settings Wizard – to save configuration details in a special file (with the extension .ops). You can then restore the details in the file as a way of transferring your PowerPoint settings to another machine, or as a backup for your existing PC.

You could save configuration details on your web site, as a handy backup.

Using the Save My Settings Wizard

1 Close PowerPoint (and all other Office programs)

2 Click Start, Programs, Microsoft Office Tools, Save My Settings Wizard

Not closing all modules can result in faulty configuration details being written.

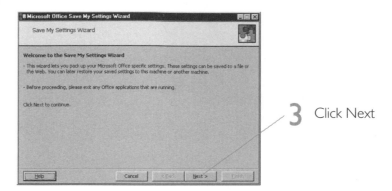

3 Click Next

4 Click Save... to save configuration details, or Restore... to implement previously saved settings

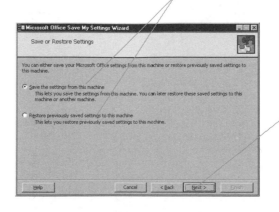

5 Click Next and complete the subsequent dialogs

Making presentations secure

You can password-protect your presentations in two ways:

- on an open basis (where users need a password to open a presentation)

- on a use basis (where users need a password to amend a presentation; without the password, they can still view it and/or save it to another name)

Setting a password

Make a written note of your password and keep it safe. If you lose it, you won't be able to access your presentation.

Perform step 3 and/or 4.

Password are case-sensitive, so make sure you enter them carefully.

You can use any permutation of letters, spaces, numbers and symbols in passwords.

1 Pull down the Tools menu and select Options

2 Ensure the Security tab is active

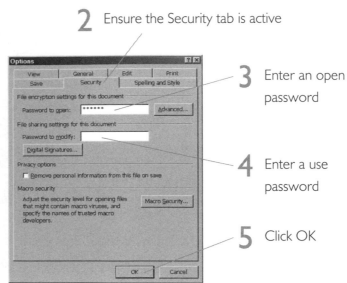

3 Enter an open password

4 Enter a use password

5 Click OK

6 Reiterate your password(s) then click OK

Opening password-protected presentations

1 Follow the relevant procedures on page 67 to open a presentation

2 PowerPoint 2002 launches a special dialog. Do the following:

3 Type in the password you set in step 3 on the facing page

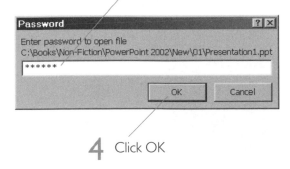

4 Click OK

Amending password-protected presentations

1 If you also set an open password, follow steps 1–4 above. If not, merely follow step 1

2 Type in the password you set in step 4 on the facing page

If a use password has been allocated to a presentation but steps 2–3 on the immediate right haven't been followed, any attempt to save alterations produces the Save As dialog.

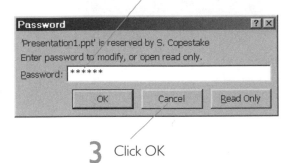

3 Click OK

Amending or removing passwords

1 Open the password-protected presentation, using the appropriate techniques on page 31

2 Follow steps 1–2 on page 30

3 Amend or delete one or more passwords

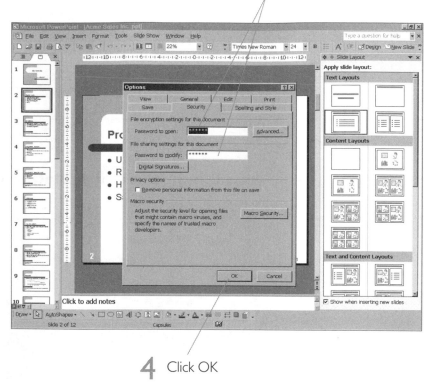

4 Click OK

5 If you amended a password in step 3, follow step 6 on page 30

Creating slide shows

In this chapter, you'll create advanced slide shows (including from the web). You'll also apply new layouts to slides, enter text via placeholders and handwrite text. Additionally, you'll create your own templates; correct text errors automatically; create text boxes; format/bullet text; search for and replace text; and then spell-check it. You'll go on to work with slide outlines and save your work to disk. Finally, you'll save your slide shows to the web/intranets as HTML files and web archives, reopen them in Internet Explorer and import data directly from Word.

Covers

Chapter Two

Creating slide shows – an overview

PowerPoint 2002 lets you create a new presentation in the following ways (in descending order of ease of use):

- with the help of the AutoContent Wizard

- by basing it on a template, and creating each slide and its contents (apart from the background) manually

- by creating a blank presentation, and creating each slide and its contents (including the background) manually

The AutoContent Wizard is a high-powered yet easy to use shortcut to creating a slide show. It incorporates a question-and-answer system. You work through a series of dialogs, answering the appropriate questions and making the relevant choices. This is the easiest way to produce a slide show, but the results are nonetheless highly professional.

When you create slide shows based on templates, you can use a shortcut. If applicable, you can simply edit the text placeholders inserted when you apply layouts (pre-defined formatting schemes), rather than create your own text boxes.
(See page 43 for how to edit existing placeholders, or page 48 for how to add and complete your own text boxes.)

Templates – also known as boilerplates – are sample presentations, complete with the relevant formatting and/or text. By basing a new slide show on a template, you automatically have access to these. Templates don't offer as many formatting choices as the AutoContent Wizard, but the results are equally as professional.

Slide shows created with the use of templates or the AutoContent Wizard can easily be amended subsequently.

Creating blank presentations is the simplest route; use this if you want to define the slide show components yourself from scratch. This is often not the most efficient or effective way to create new presentations. However, it isn't as onerous as might be imagined because PowerPoint 2002 lets you apply the following:

- pre-defined slide layouts (to individual slides) – see the tip

- slide designs based on templates (see Chapter 3)

Using the AutoContent Wizard

When you use the AutoContent wizard, you create a presentation which contains pre-defined content and design elements (although you can easily change as many of these as you want later). You can also choose from a large number of presentation types; these are organised under several headings (e.g. General, Corporate and Projects) and are suitable for most purposes.

Launching the AutoContent Wizard

1   Pull down the File menu and do the following:

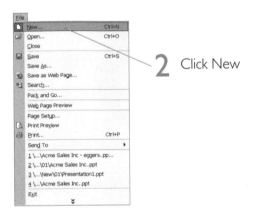

2   Click New

You can also create new slide shows directly from existing ones. In this way, PowerPoint copies the original; you can then make the necessary changes and save it under a new name.

On the Task Pane, click Choose Presentation. Use the New from Existing Presentation dialog to locate and double-click the slide show to be copied. Make the relevant amendments and save it to a new name (File, Save As).

3   Select From AutoContent Wizard

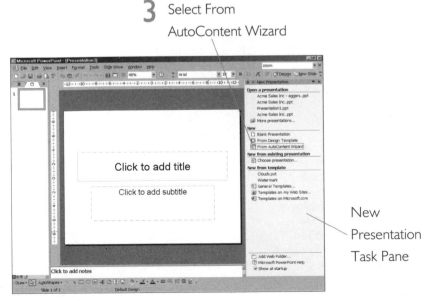

New
Presentation
Task Pane

...cont'd

If you want help with the AutoContent wizard, consider turning on the Office Assistant before running it. To do this, pull down the Help menu and click Show Office Assistant.

The Office Assistant may be annoying, but it does provide help with using the wizard

AutoContent Wizard

The AutoContent Wizard will create 8 to 12 slides with suggested content that you can change.

The AutoContent wizard uses content templates. These are design templates with the addition of a suggested outline.

To add your own template to the wizard, follow step 5. Click Add. Use the Select Presentation Template to locate and double-click the relevant template. Now select it in step 6, if you want.

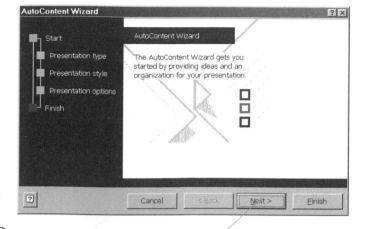

4 Click here

5 Click a slide show heading

6 Click a slide show type

7 Click Next

Re step 8 – To have PowerPoint 2002 apply a colour scheme which is suitable for use on the Internet or intranets, select Web presentation.
(For more on colour schemes, see Chapter 3.)

8 Select an output type

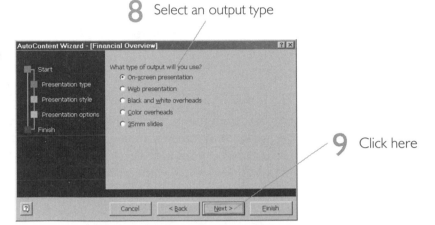

9 Click here

10 Type in slide text

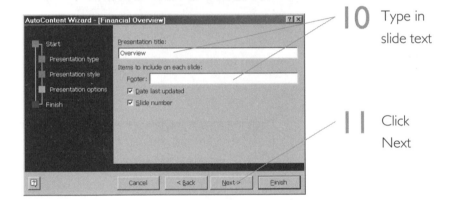

11 Click Next

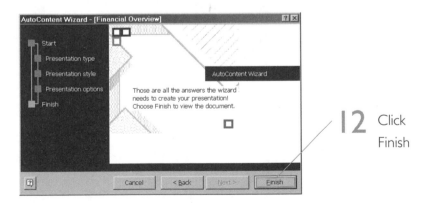

12 Click Finish

Using templates

Note that, with some layouts, you can also add the following:

- *pictures/clip art (see chapter 6)*
- *org charts (see chapter 6), and/or;*
- *charts (see chapter 5)*

When you create a slide show with the help of a template, you:

1. select a template

2. apply a pre-defined layout

3. type in the textual content (but see the DON'T FORGET tip)

Step 1 applies to the overall presentation, while steps 2 and 3 have to be undertaken for every individual slide. This makes creating new presentations based on templates a rather longer process than using the AutoContent Wizard. However, the end result is likely to be more personalised, and it is easier to have variations in individual style layout, if you need this.

Creating a new slide show based on a template

Pull down the File menu and click New

2 Select General Templates

You can also base your presentation on templates on other websites. Click Templates on my Web Sites and follow the on-screen instructions.

Additionally, you can base your slide show on extra templates provided by Microsoft. Click Templates on Microsoft.com and follow the on-screen instructions.

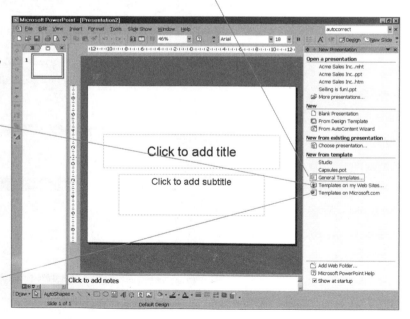

You can use the dialog shown on the right to create a new slide show optimised for use on intranets.

Follow steps 1–2 on the facing page. In step 3 on the right, activate the Presentations tab (then ignore the remaining steps). Double-click this icon:

Group Home Page

3 Double-click a template

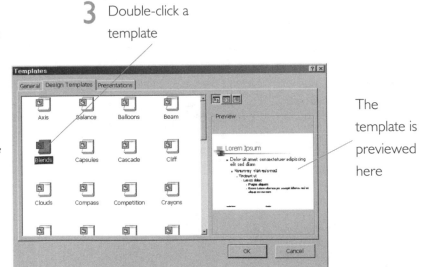

The template is previewed here

Applying a layout to the new slide show

For more on using design templates, see chapter 3.

If you want to keep the default title layout, omit step 4 and jump to step 5.

You have to repeat step 4 for every new slide you add (see overleaf).

4 Select a layout

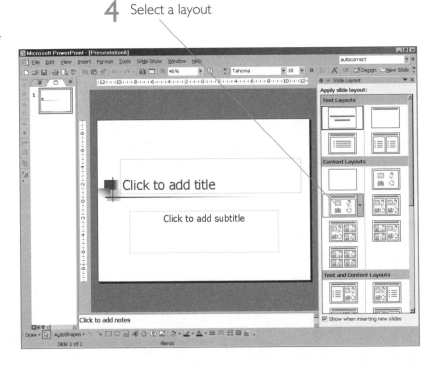

The Title slide for the new presentation is shown below:

This is a content placeholder — see chapter 6 for how to use it:

Text placeholder

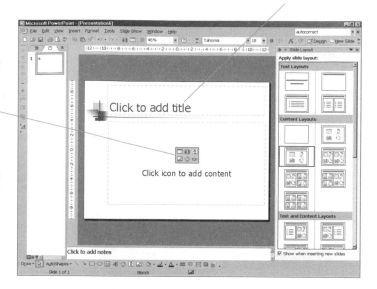

You can create your own templates for future use. When saved, they appear in the Slide Design Task Pane (Format, Slide Design).

Open the slide show you want to preserve. Choose File, Save As. In the Save as type: field, select Design Template (*.pot). Select a drive/folder then name the template. Click Save.

5 Click in the text placeholder and type in the necessary text (for more information on how to do this, see page 43).

Creating additional slides

Pull down the Insert menu and do the following to create a new slide based on the template you selected in step 3 on page 39:

After steps 1– 2 or 3, follow steps 4–5 on page 39 to assign a slide layout.

Repeat the procedures described under 'Creating additional slides' for as many new slides as you want to insert.

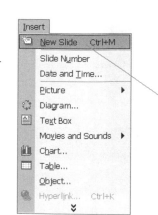

2 Click New Slide

3 Alternatively, omit steps 1–2. Instead, just press Ctrl+M

Creating blank slide shows

Follow step 1 on page 38

You can insert slides from an external slide show into the active one.

Select the slide you want to precede the new one. Pull down the Insert menu and click Slides from Files. Locate the presentation you want to copy from then specify the relevant slides. Click Insert (or Insert All to insert all slides).

2 Select Blank Presentation

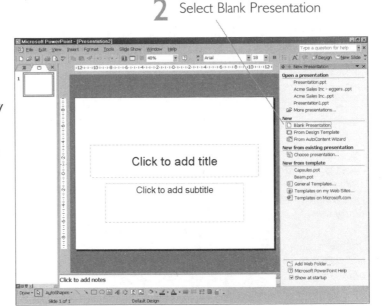

3 Select a layout

When you've finished filling in the Title slide, follow the procedures under 'Creating additional slides' on the facing page to:

- *add new slides*
- *assign layouts to them, and;*
- *insert text in the relevant placeholders*

4 Using any text placeholders, type in the necessary text

Customising slide structure

Once you've created a slide show (using any of the methods discussed earlier), the easiest way to customise the basic format of a slide is to add a layout to it. There are over 20 layout structures and you can apply your choice to a specific slide or group of slides. You can then amend the individual components (see later topics).

Adding layouts

You can select more than one slide in Slide Sorter view by holding down Shift as you click on the slide icons.

1 Make sure you're in Normal, Slide Sorter or Thumbnail view (see page 15 for how to switch between views). If you're in Slide Sorter or Thumbnail view, select the slide(s) you want to amend

You can also customise slide shows by applying design templates – see chapter 3.

2 Pull down the Format menu and click Slide Layout

3 Click a layout

Any slide components present before you applied the new layout will still remain (however, PowerPoint may well rearrange or resize them). This is a feature called AutoLayout in action. If you don't want this, you can disable it. Choose Tools, AutoCorrect Options. In the AutoCorrect... dialog, select the AutoFormat As You Type tab and untick Automatic layout for inserted objects. Click OK.

Use standard mouse techniques to reposition or rescale text objects in PowerPoint 2002.

Adding text to slides

When you create a new slide show (with one exception – see the DON'T FORGET tip), PowerPoint 2002 fills each slide with placeholders containing sample text. The idea is that you should replace this with your own text.

The illustration below shows a sample slide before customisation:

If you choose to assign a blank layout to one or more slides, no text placeholders will be present. (Instead, follow the procedures on page 48 to insert one or more text boxes.)

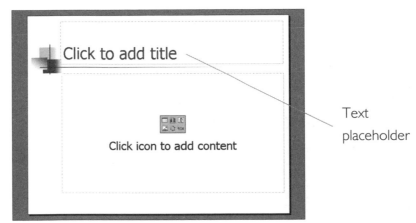

Click to add title

Click icon to add content

Text placeholder

Inserting text into a text placeholder is a shortcut to the creation of a text box.

To insert your own text, click in any text placeholder. PowerPoint displays a text entry box. Do the following:

When you enter text into a placeholder, PowerPoint 2002 resizes it to fit. It does this by altering:

- the line spacing
- the type size, or;
- both

This is PowerPoint's AutoFit feature in action – see also page 52.

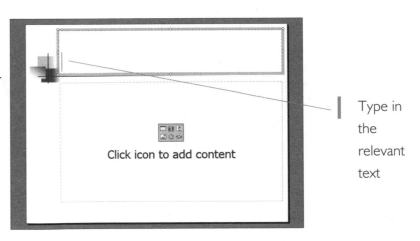

Click icon to add content

Type in the relevant text

2 Finally, click anywhere outside the placeholder to confirm the addition of the new text.

Handwriting text

To use handwriting recognition for the first time, you have to perform a custom install. Do this in the usual way but select Office Shared Features/Alternative User Input in Office's installer.

You can handwrite text into a pad and have PowerPoint convert it into standard text. You can also enter text via a virtual keyboard.

If the Language Bar isn't visible or minimised on the Taskbar, go to Control Panel. Double-click Text Services. In the dialog, click Language Bar. Select Show the Language bar on the desktop. Click OK twice. Now maximise the Language Bar, if necessary

You can import handwritten notes made on a Handheld or Pocket PC into PowerPoint – see the device's documentation.

2 Click Handwriting   3 Select Writing Pad

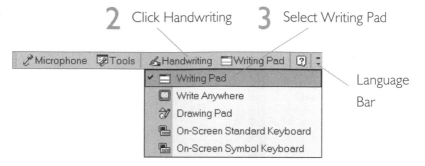

Language Bar

Re step 3 – click Write Anywhere to write directly on-screen, or On-Screen Standard Keyboard to use a virtual keyboard to enter text.

You can write with special devices (e.g. graphics tablets) or with the mouse.

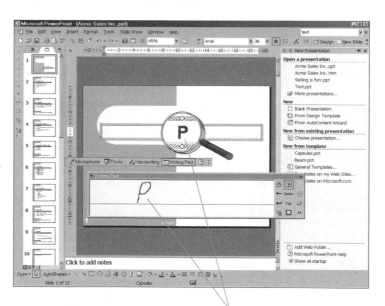

By default, PowerPoint converts data to text. However, you enter it as handwriting (which can be formatted in the normal way). Click this button in the Writing Pad:

4 Handwrite data on the line in the Writing Pad (don't pause between letters/digits but do leave appropriate spaces) – PowerPoint enters the data as soon as it recognizes it

AutoCorrect – an overview

AutoCorrect is a very useful PowerPoint 2002 feature. Its principal purpose is to correct typing errors automatically. It does this by maintaining a list of inaccurate spellings and their corrected versions. When you press the Spacebar or Enter/Return keys immediately after making a mistake, the correction is substituted for the original error.

AutoCorrect is supplied with a long list of preset corrections. These are examples:

- 'allwasy' and 'allwyas' become 'always'

- 'acomodate and 'acommodate' become 'accommodate'

- 'alot' becomes 'a lot'

- 'dont' becomes 'don't'

- 'garantee' becomes 'guarantee'

- 'oppertunity' becomes 'opportunity'

- 'wierd' becomes 'weird'

In addition, however, you can easily define your own. If, for instance, you regularly type 'lthe' when you mean 'the', you can have AutoCorrect make the correction for you.

You can also enter shortened forms of correct words – or entire phrases – and have them expanded automatically. (For instance, you could have AutoCorrect expand 'ann' into 'Annual Profit Forecast'...)

AutoCorrect has further uses. You can have:

1. the first letters of sentences capitalised

2. words which begin with two capitals corrected (e.g. 'HEllo' becomes 'Hello')

3. days capitalised (e.g. 'monday' becomes 'Monday')

Customising AutoCorrect

You can add new corrections, delete existing ones or specify which AutoCorrect functions are active.

Adding new corrections

Pull down the Tools menu and do the following:

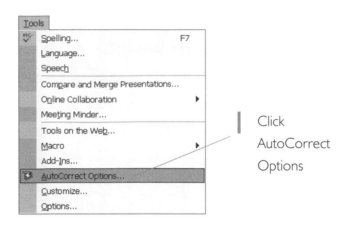

1 Click AutoCorrect Options

2 Select the AutoCorrect tab

3 Type in the incorrect word

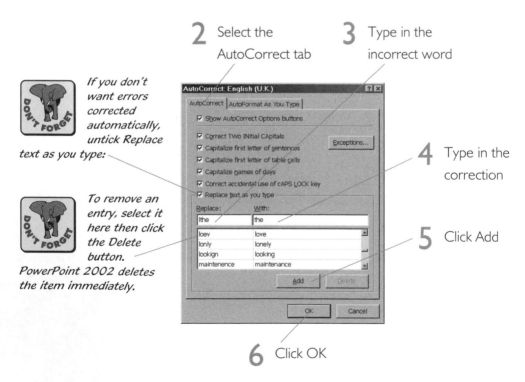

If you don't want errors corrected automatically, untick Replace text as you type:

To remove an entry, select it here then click the Delete button.
PowerPoint 2002 deletes the item immediately.

4 Type in the correction

5 Click Add

6 Click OK

Setting other AutoCorrect options

1 Carry out step 1 on the facing page.

An exception is a letter or word (followed by a full stop) after which you don't want the first letter of the following word capitalised.

2 Select the AutoCorrect tab

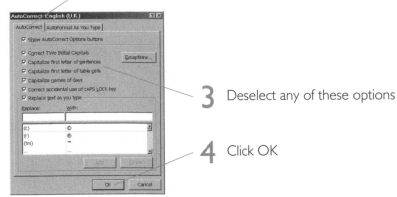

3 Deselect any of these options

4 Click OK

Re step 2 – you can also specify exceptions to the rule whereby double capitals at the start of words are corrected. For example, the plural of the abbreviation PA (for Personal Assistant) is 'PAs'. Clearly, for PowerPoint to correct this to 'Pas' would be wrong.

Select the INitial CAps tab. Enter the exception in the Don't correct field and click Add. Click OK twice.

Specifying exceptions

There are situations where automatic capitalisation is wrong. For instance, if you type in 'approx.' followed by another word, the first letter of the second word is incorrectly capitalised due to the preceding full stop. To prevent this, you can set up an exception.

1 In the above dialog, click this button: Exceptions...

2 Select the First Letter tab

3 Type in an exception

This dialog does not distinguish between lower- and upper-case. For example, entering 'quart.' has the same effect as entering 'Quart.' or 'QUART.'.

4 Click Add

5 Click OK, then click OK in the AutoCorrect... dialog

Inserting text boxes

If a slide contains no text placeholders, you can still insert text easily and conveniently by creating and inserting a text box.

Creating a text box

Refer to the Drawing toolbar. (If it isn't on-screen, pull down the View menu and click Toolbars, Drawing.) Do the following:

This way of defining a text box ensures that the text you enter subsequently is subject to wrap (i.e. surplus text automatically moves to the next line).

If you don't want this, follow step 1. Omit steps 2–3. Then click where you want the text to appear and begin typing immediately. PowerPoint 2002 extends the containing text box to ensure that the text stays on the original line.

Click here

You can also use text boxes in charts – see page 119.

2 Move the mouse cursor over the slide and position it where you want the text box to begin. Drag to define the text box

3 Type in the relevant text. Press Enter when you've finished

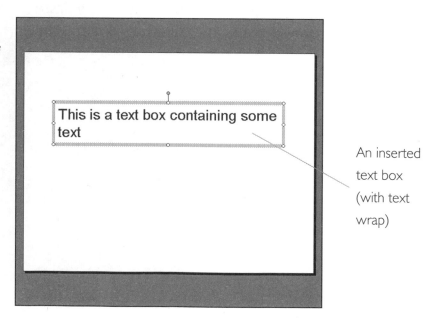

This is a text box containing some text

An inserted text box (with text wrap)

Formatting text

You can carry out a variety of formatting enhancements on text. You can:

- change the font and/or type size

- apply a font style or effect

- apply a colour

- specify the alignment and/or line spacing

- insert tabs/indents

- apply/modify bullets

Font-based formatting

Click inside the relevant text object then select the text you want to format. Pull down the Format menu and click Font. Carry out any of steps 1–6 below, as appropriate. Then follow step 7:

Re step 4 – styles you can apply are Bold, Italic and Bold/ Italic.

(Depending on the font selected in step 1, not all of them may be available.)

You can launch the Font dialog by pressing Ctrl+T.

Re step 6 – if none of the colours here are suitable, click More Colors. In the new dialog, click a colour in the polygon in the centre. Then click OK. Finally, follow step 7.

1 Click a new typeface

2 Type in a new point size

7 Click here

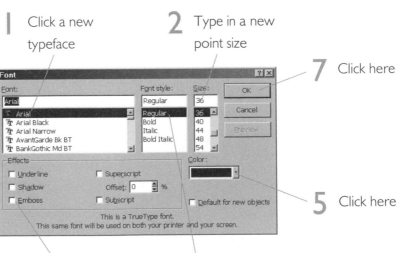

5 Click here

3 Tick any effect to apply it

4 Click a font style

6 Click a colour (see the HOT TIP)

The following are some examples of line spacing in action:

This is single
line spacing
This is 1.5
line spacing
This is double
line spacing

Changing text spacing

First, click inside the relevant text object and select the text whose spacing you want to amend. Pull down the Format menu and click Line Spacing. Now carry out any of steps 1–3 below, as appropriate. Then follow step 4.

1 Type in a line spacing

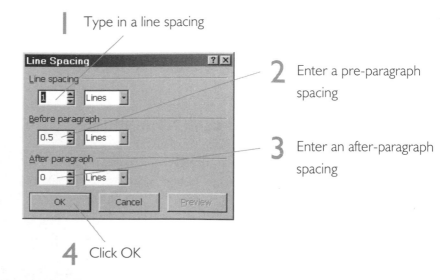

2 Enter a pre-paragraph spacing

3 Enter an after-paragraph spacing

4 Click OK

The following are some examples of alignment in action:

This is left alignment
This is centre alignment
This is right alignment
This is justification – text aligns to the left *and* right

Changing text alignment

First, click inside the relevant text object and select the text whose alignment you want to amend. Pull down the Format menu and do the following:

1 Click Alignment

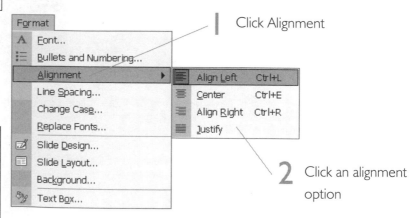

2 Click an alignment option

You can also use the following alignment shortcuts:

Ctrl+L	Left-align
Ctrl+E	Centre-align
Ctrl+R	Right-align

If the ruler isn't currently visible, pull down the View menu and click Ruler.

Applying tabs

First, click inside the relevant text object. Ensure the ruler is on-screen. Now do the following:

| Click where you want the tab stop to appear

To delete a tab stop, simply drag it (the 'L' shape) off the ruler.

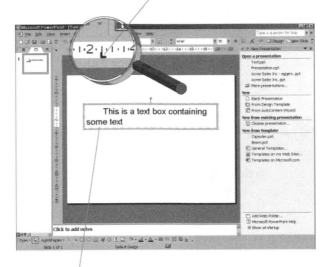

Here, step 2 has forced the first line to the right

Never use the Space bar to indent text: spaces vary in size according to the typeface and type size applying, and therefore give uneven results.

2 Back in the text, click where you want the tab to take effect and press the Tab key

Applying indents

First, click inside the relevant text object. Ensure the ruler is on-screen. Now do the following, as appropriate:

Re step 2 on the right – drag the square component:

Here

to revise the indent for all lines equally.

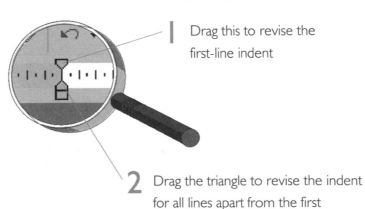

| Drag this to revise the first-line indent

2 Drag the triangle to revise the indent for all lines apart from the first

Bulleting text

Using a feature called AutoFit, PowerPoint automatically shrinks text as you type so that it fits on the host slide. However, you can control the process because a Smart Tag appears:

Click here then select an option

· Text in slides is often bulleted, for increased impact:

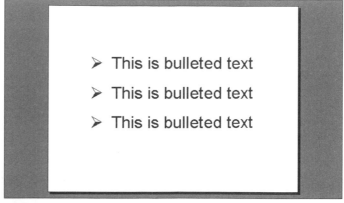

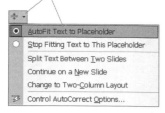

You can reverse the AutoFit, continue on a new slide or split the text into columns.

Adding bullets to text

To number text lines, follow steps 1–2. Activate the Numbered tab. In the dialog, double-click a number system.

1 Click in the relevant text block and select the text you want to reformat

2 Pull down the Format menu and click Bullets and Numbering

3 Activate the Bulleted tab

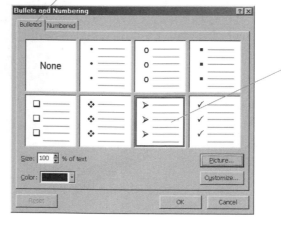

4 Double-click a bullet

If none of the standard bullets are suitable, omit step 4. Instead, click the Customize button. In the Font: field in the Symbol dialog, select a font. In the body of the dialog, double-click the character you want to use as a bullet.

5 To start a new unbulleted/unnumbered line, press Shift+Enter

Working with slide outlines

If you prefer, you can disable AutoFit (see the HOT TIP on the facing page).

Choose Tools, AutoCorrect Options. In the AutoCorrect dialog, select the AutoFormat As You Type tab and untick AutoFit title text to placeholder and/or AutoFit body text to placeholder. Click OK.

You can use the Outline component of Normal view (called Outline view) to organize and develop the content of your presentation.

In Outline view, you can:

- build presentation structures

- move entire slides from one position to another

- edit text entries

- hide or display text levels

Creating a presentation structure

First create a presentation, using any of the methods discussed earlier in this chapter. If necessary, pull down the View menu and click Normal. Now carry out step 1 below:

Before step 1, ensure the Outline tab is selected:

Click a slide entry

This is the Outline toolbar: and this is Outline view:

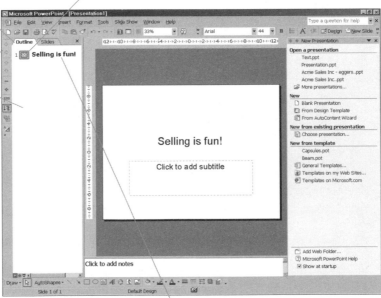

After step 2, Outline view looks something like this:

In other words, a second slide has been created. To demote this to a bulleted entry, see overleaf.

2 Type in title text and press Enter (the change is reflected in the slide itself) to create a new level

If the Outlining toolbar isn't on-screen, pull down the View menu and click Toolbars, Outlining.

'Demoting' a text entry moves it to a lower level.

If you need to 'promote' a text entry (i.e. move it to a higher level), click in it. Then click this button in the Outlining toolbar:

3 Refer to the Outlining toolbar and do the following:

4 Click here to demote the 2nd slide to a sub-entry in the first

5 Type in sub-text and press Enter. Repeat as often as necessary

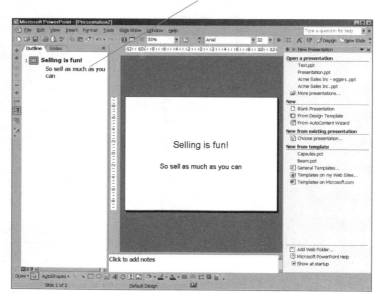

6 When you've finished with the first slide, press Ctrl+Enter to jump to the next. Use the earlier techniques to add text to this. Repeat these procedures for as many slides as you want to include

Moving slides

To reposition slides in Outline view, carry out the following steps:

Re step 1 – to select multiple slides in Outline view, hold down one Shift key as you click their markers.

1 | Click a slide marker

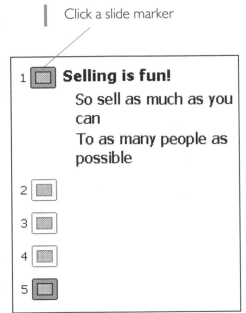

You can also move demoted entries *within* slides or to other slides.

Ignore step 1. Triple-click a demoted entry (e.g. 'So sell as much as you can'). In step 2, move the entry to a new level within the original slide or to a new one.

2 | Drag the slide to a new location in the Outline tree

You can combine both procedures described here. For instance, if you drag a demoted entry to a new blank slide, PowerPoint promotes it to a title...

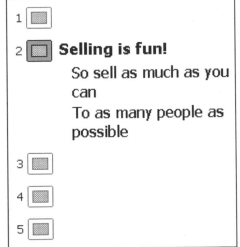

3 | What was previously slide 1 is now slide 2...

You can collect titles on specified slides and insert them into a new slide.

In Outline view, select the relevant slides by holding down Shift as you click their marker:

in the Outline tree. Then click the Summary Slide button:

in the Outlining toolbar. PowerPoint inserts the new slide in front of the 1st selected slide.

Hiding/displaying entries

An important feature of PowerPoint 2002's Outline view is the ability to hide or reveal entries at will. This enables you to alternate between achieving a useful overview and viewing entries in detail. Do the following:

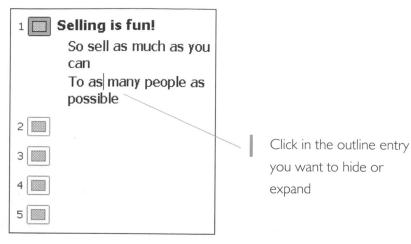

Click in the outline entry you want to hide or expand

2 In the Outlining toolbar, click to hide the entry OR to expand it

To edit a text entry, simply click in it. Then use standard Windows text editing techniques.

Click outside the entry when you've finished.

3 The underlining denotes that the sub-entries in the example above have now been (temporarily) hidden

The process of hiding entries is called 'collapsing'. Expanding is the reverse.

4 Optional – to re-hide or re-expand an entry, repeat step 2 as appropriate. Or double-click its marker

Searching for text

PowerPoint 2002 lets you search for specific text within a slide show. For example, you can if you want have PowerPoint 2002 locate (successively) all instances of the word 'Money'.

You can also:

- limit the search to words which match the case of the text you specify (e.g. if you search for 'Sales', PowerPoint 2002 will not go to slides which contain 'sales' or 'SALES')

- limit the search to whole words (e.g. if you search for 'pound', PowerPoint 2002 will not find slides which contain 'pounds')

Initiating a text search

Pull down the Edit menu and click Find. Now do the following:

1 Type in the text you want to find

3 Click here to start the search

To restrict a find operation to specific text, select it before steps 1–3.

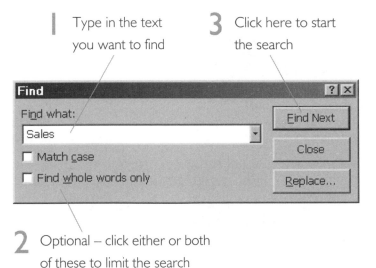

2 Optional – click either or both of these to limit the search

Step 3 locates the first instance of the search text; repeat it to locate the next. And so on…

Replacing text

When you've located text, you can have PowerPoint 2002 replace it automatically (or one instance at a time) with the text of your choice.

To restrict a replace operation to specific text, select it before steps 1–4.

When you undertake a find-and-replace operation, you can (as with find operations) make the search component case-specific, or limit it to whole-word matches. (See page 57 for illustrations of both of these restrictions.)

Initiating a find-and-replace operation

First pull down the Edit menu and click Replace. Now follow steps 1 and 2 below. Finally, follow either step 3 OR 4:

1 Type in the text you want to find

2 Type in the replacement text

Before you begin replacing text, specify any parameters you need here:

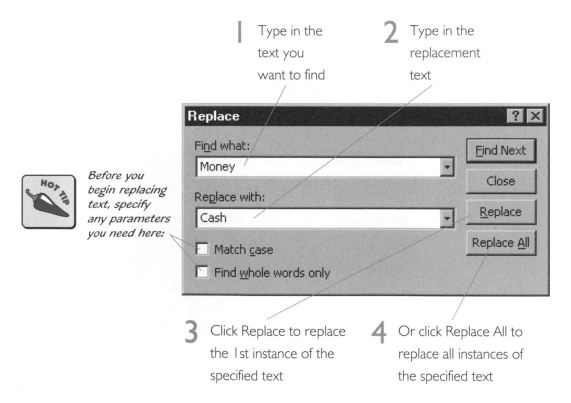

3 Click Replace to replace the 1st instance of the specified text

4 Or click Replace All to replace all instances of the specified text

Spell-checking

PowerPoint 2002 lets you check text in two ways:

- on-the-fly, as you type in text

- separately, after the text has been entered

Checking text on-the-fly

This is the default. When automatic checking is in force, PowerPoint 2002 flags words it doesn't recognise, using a red underline. If the word or phrase is wrong, right-click in it. Then carry out steps 1, 2, 3 OR 4:

Re step 2 – following this ensures that the word is ignored in this checking session only.
(To ignore it forever, carry out step 3 instead.)

Re step 3 – PowerPoint maintains a special dictionary (called CUSTOM.DIC). Carry out step 3 if:

- *the flagged word is correct, and;*
- *you want PowerPoint to remember it in future spell-checks (by adding it to your user dictionary)*

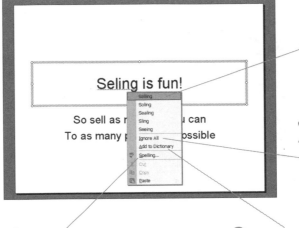

1 If an alternative is correct, click it to substitute it for the wrong version

2 Click Ignore All if you want the flagged word to stand

3 Click Add to Dictionary to have the word added to your user dictionary

4 If the flagged word is wrong but can't be corrected now, click Spelling and complete the resulting dialog (see page 60)

Disabling on-the-fly checking

Re step 2 on the immediate right – if you want to keep spell-checking on-the-fly but without printing the red lines, tick Hide all spelling errors instead.

1 Pull down the Tools menu and click Options

2 Activate the Spelling and Style tab in the Options dialog, then deselect Check spelling as you type

3 Click OK

To check text in another language, select the text then choose Tools, Language. In the Language dialog, select a new language and click OK. Now press F7 to begin the spell-check.

Re step 1 – if none of the suggestions are correct, type the correct word in the Change to: field then follow step 2.

PowerPoint makes use of two separate dictionaries. One – CUSTOM.DIC – is yours. When you click the Add button (see the tip below), the flagged word is stored in CUSTOM.DIC and recognised in future checking sessions.

You have two further spelling-related options. These are:

- *Click Add to store the flagged word in CUSTOM.DIC, or;*

- *Click Change All to substitute the suggestion for all future instances of the flagged word (but only in this checking session)*

Checking text separately

To check all the text within the active slide show in one go, pull down the Tools menu and click Spelling. PowerPoint 2002 starts spell-checking the presentation from the present location. When it encounters a word or phrase it doesn't recognise, PowerPoint flags it and produces a special dialog (see below). Usually, it provides alternative suggestions; if one of these is correct, you can opt to have it replace the flagged word. You can do this singly (i.e. just this instance is replaced) or globally (where all future instances – within the current checking session – are replaced).

Alternatively, you can have PowerPoint ignore *this* instance of the flagged word, ignore *all* future instances of the word or add the word to CUSTOM.DIC (see the HOT TIPS). After this, PowerPoint resumes checking.

Carry out step 1 below, then follow step 2. Alternatively, carry out step 3 or 4.

1 If one of the suggestions here is correct, click it, then follow step 2

3 Click Ignore to ignore just this instance

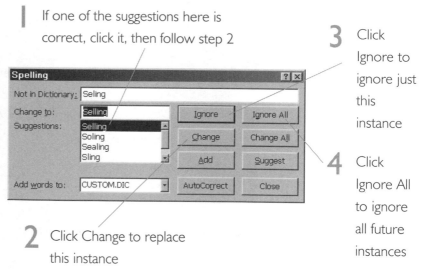

2 Click Change to replace this instance

4 Click Ignore All to ignore all future instances

Saving slide shows

It's important to save your work at frequent intervals, in order to avoid data loss in the event of a hardware fault or power interruption.

Saving a presentation for the first time

Pull down the File menu and click Save. Or press Ctrl+S. Now do the following:

2 Click here. In the drop-down list, click a drive/folder combination

Re step 2 – click any buttons here: for access to the relevant folders.

(For instance, to save files to your Desktop, click Desktop.)

Re step 1 – to save slide shows to third-party formats or as graphics files, select the relevant format. If a message launches, specify whether you want to save all the slides or just the active one.

(If you export to graphics files, all relevant slides are saved as separate images in the folder you specify.)

Note that you can use a shortcut for either save method.

Click this icon:

in the Standard toolbar.

3 Type in a file name

4 Click Save

Click here. In the list, click the format you want to save to

Saving previously saved presentations

1 Pull down the File menu and click Save

2 Or press Ctrl+S

3 Either way, no dialog launches; instead, PowerPoint 2002 saves the latest version of your slide show to disk, overwriting the previous one

Web publishing – an overview

Preliminaries

You can save presentations – usually in HTML (HyperText Markup Language) format – to network, web or FTP servers. You can do this so long as you've created a shortcut to the appropriate folder.

With regard to HTML, the above actions are possible because, with PowerPoint 2000, Microsoft redefined its HTML format.

HTML enhancements

The standard web format (*.html or *.htm) incorporates the following:

- it's a Companion File format (Microsoft regards it as occupying the same status as its proprietary formats); this means that you can create *and* share rich web documents with the same PowerPoint 2002 tools used to create printed documents

- it duplicates the functionality of the proprietary formats (i.e. all the usual PowerPoint 2002 features are preserved when saving in HTML format)

- it's recognised by the Windows Clipboard. This means that data can be copied from Internet Explorer and pasted directly into PowerPoint 2002

Types of web saving

PowerPoint 2002 lets you work with two main types of web page:

HTML files

You can publish presentation as standard HTML files in the usual way. These files have all the benefits listed above.

Web archives

Web archives are special aggregate HTML files which:

- combine and unify all web site elements (text and pictures)

- can be published or sent via email as just one file

Web archives have the extension *.mht or *.mhtml.

Creating shortcuts

In order to save web-format documents to network, web or FTP servers, you need to have created a shortcut to the relevant folder.

Creating shortcuts to web/FTP folders

1 Open the Open (File, Open) or Export... (File, Export) dialog and do the following:

3 Double-click Add Web Folder

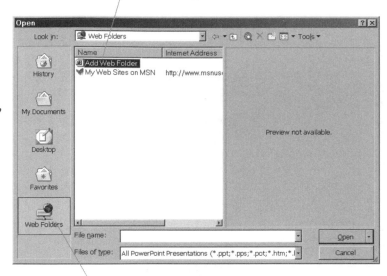

2 In Windows NT 4 or 98, click here

4 Follow the on-screen instructions

Creating shortcuts to local network folders

This requires a different procedure.

Windows 2000/Me users should use My Network Places, while Windows NT 4.0 and 98 users should use Network Neighborhood. (For how to do this, see your system administrator.)

Publishing to the web

Previewing your work before saving

Pull down the File menu and do the following:

Click Web Page Preview

Before you can save files to web folders or FTP sites, you must first have carried out the relevant procedures. See page 63.

Your browser now launches, with your work displayed in it. To close it when you've finished using it, press Alt+F4.

Publishing presentations – the quick route

Pull down the File menu and click Save as Web Page. Then do the following:

Re step 1 – carry out one of the following procedures according to which version of Windows you're running:

* *Windows NT 4 and 98 users – use Network Neighborhood to save to a local network folder and Web Folders to save to a web or FTP folder*

* *Windows 2000 and Me users – use My Network Places to save to a local network folder or to a web or FTP folder*

1 Click here. In the list, select a recipient (see the HOT TIP)

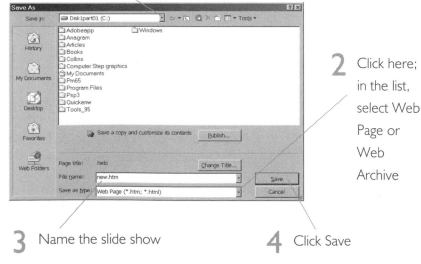

2 Click here; in the list, select Web Page or Web Archive

3 Name the slide show

4 Click Save

Publishing presentations – the detailed route

On the facing page, we looked at how to save a presentation to the web with the minimum of preparation. However, you can also use a slightly different route which lets you customise how the slide show is saved. You can:

- specify whether the whole presentation is published

- if not, select which slides should be published

- opt to exclude speaker notes

- aim the presentation at specific browsers (or at all browsers – this produces bigger files)

- set detailed web options

1 Pull down the File menu and click Save as Web Page

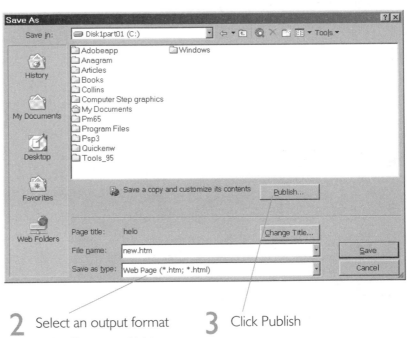

2 Select an output format (Web Page... or Web Archive...)

3 Click Publish

...cont'd

To set web options, click Web Options. Complete the dialog.

You can use the Open dialog (see the facing page) to create a new slide show based on Microsoft Word, RTF or text files.

Word and RTF files	The new presentation's outline is structured hierarchically by heading styles
Text files	The outline is structured hierarchically by tabs

In the Files of type: field, select All Outlines... Double-click the file you want to base the new presentation on.

(You'll probably need to revise the new slide show.)

If you're using Word 2002, you can send text directly to PowerPoint; when you do this, you create a new presentation (but, as above, you'll probably have to edit it fairly extensively).

In Word, choose File, Send To, Microsoft PowerPoint.

4 Select Complete presentation or specify slides to include

5 Select a browser option

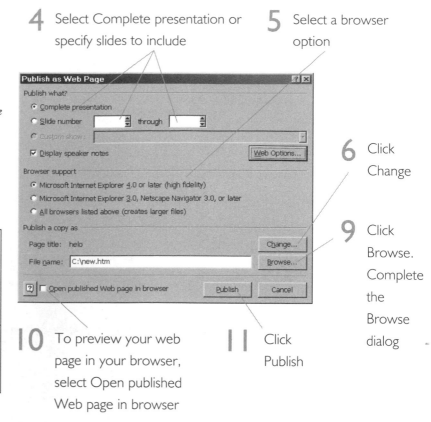

6 Click Change

9 Click Browse. Complete the Browse dialog

10 To preview your web page in your browser, select Open published Web page in browser

11 Click Publish

7 Name the presentation (this appears in the browser's title bar)

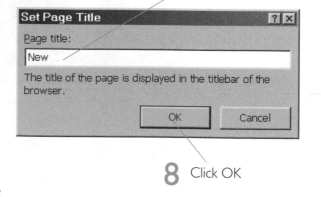

8 Click OK

Opening slide shows

We saw earlier that you can create new presentations in PowerPoint. You can also open PowerPoint 2002 presentations you've already created.

Refer to the Task Pane on the right of the screen and perform steps 1–2 (if you haven't recently opened the presentation you want to open, carry out steps 3–4 instead):

If the Task Pane isn't visible, choose View, Task Pane.

To open a web- or intranet-based slide show, right-click any toolbar and select Web. In the Web toolbar, click the Go button and select Open Hyperlink in the menu. In the Open Internet Address dialog, type in the presentation's address and name. Click OK.

You can also launch the Open dialog directly from within PowerPoint. Press Ctrl+O.

You can copy, rename or delete presentations from within the Open dialog.
Right-click any presentation entry in the main part of the dialog. In the menu, click the desired option. Now carry out the appropriate action.
An example: to rename a presentation, click Rename in the menu. Type in the new name and press Enter.

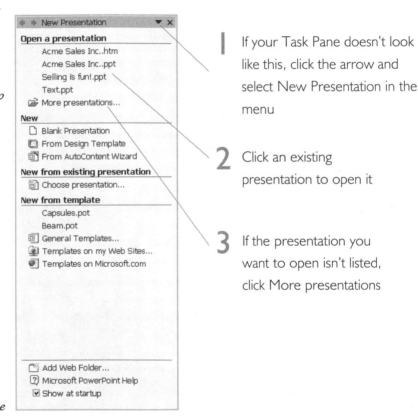

1 If your Task Pane doesn't look like this, click the arrow and select New Presentation in the menu

2 Click an existing presentation to open it

3 If the presentation you want to open isn't listed, click More presentations

4 Use the Open dialog to:

- select a file type (you can also open slide shows in third-party formats)
- locate and double-click the presentation you want to open

Reopening HTML files

See pages 62–66 for how to generate HTML files from PowerPoint 2002 presentations.

Because Microsoft regards HTML as having the same status as its own proprietary formats, when you export HTML files in PowerPoint 2002 they can be edited directly from within Internet Explorer 5.x or later with little or no loss of data or formatting. PowerPoint calls this process 'round-tripping'.

The lack of deterioration can be demonstrated further with the help of examples. Study the two illustrations below:

You can edit PowerPoint-produced HTML files directly from within Internet Explorer 5.x or higher. Click this button in the toolbar:

PowerPoint automatically opens the HTML file.

The original slide show...

Here, there are no appreciable differences between the before and after files.

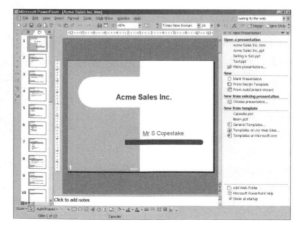

The HTML file after being reopened in PowerPoint 2002

You can also open web archive files in Internet Explorer 5.x or higher, but they have a different layout to the original PowerPoint file.

Slide design

In this chapter, you'll fine-tune the appearance of slides. You'll learn how to use masters to ensure your presentations and handouts/notes have a consistent look, then add new masters and carry out master housekeeping (renaming, protecting, duplicating and deleting masters, and restoring master placeholders). You'll also apply and change/delete colour schemes; copy them between slides with Format Painter; and apply design templates – all these techniques promote consistency.

Finally, you'll add new slide backgrounds and amend headers and footers in slide and handouts/notes.

Covers

Chapter Three

Customising slides – an overview

PowerPoint 2002 provides several methods you can use to enhance slide appearance quickly and conveniently. You can:

- customise Slide masters

- customise Title masters

- apply a new colour scheme

- apply design templates

Slide masters

Slide masters are control slides which determine the format and position of all titles and text on slides (but see the BEWARE tip). You can also insert other objects – e.g. pictures – onto a Slide master; when you do this, they're reproduced (unless you change this) on all slides *after* the first. In this way, if you want a picture – for instance, a company logo – to appear on every slide except the first, you can simply insert it on the Slide master.

In this way, masters are like word processor styles: changes to the master automatically ripple through the rest of the slide show.

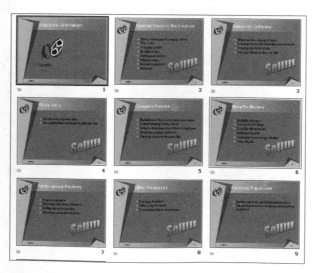

has been added to the master and appears on every slide but the first

Title masters

Title masters perform the same function as Slide masters, but only in respect of the Title (first) slide.

Handout masters

You can include the following in Handout masters and have them appear on handouts:

See Chapter 8 for how to work with Handout and Notes masters.

- pictures
- text
- headers/footers
- date/time information
- page numbers

When you add a new design template, you automatically insert a new master. For this reason, if you want to implement a presentation-wide change, you'll need to change each master (or master pair, if you're also using the title master).

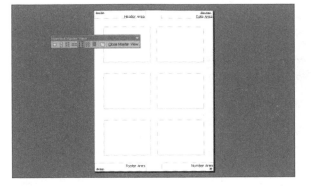

The Handout master

Title masters share some styles (formatting features) in common with slide masters.

Notes masters

You can include the same components in Notes masters to have them appear on notes.

The Notes master

Colour schemes

Colour schemes are integrated collections of colours which are guaranteed to complement each other. Each colour scheme contains eight balanced colours which are automatically applied to slide elements such as:

Colour schemes are tailor-made for the design template which hosts them.

- text

- backgrounds

- fills

You can apply colour schemes to individual slides, or to the whole of a presentation.

You can also create and use your own colour schemes.

If you plan to work on both the Slide and Title masters, work on the Slide master first (because text formatting changes on the Slide master are automatically mirrored in the Title master).

Design templates

Design templates – otherwise known simply as designs – are collections of:

- Slide masters (and often Title masters)

- colour schemes

- specific fonts which complement other elements in the design

When you apply a design template, any objects you've already applied to the Slide master (e.g. pictures or text boxes) remain.

When you apply a design template to a slide show (or to specific slides within it), it takes precedence over the existing Slide master, Title master and colour scheme. This means that when you create new slides, they automatically assume the characteristics of the new design template, irrespective of any layouts you may have applied previously.

Summary

Appropriate editing of Slide/Title masters (or the application of a new colour scheme) represents a convenient technique for ensuring your slide show has a uniform appearance and/or content. Applying a new design template is a way of doing both at the same time.

Working with masters

Editing masters is easy and convenient.

Launching masters
Pull down the View menu and do the following:

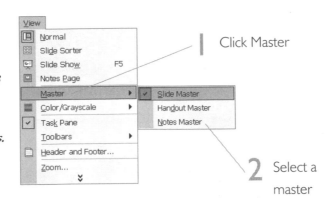

| Click Master

See Chapter 8 for how to launch the Handout and Notes masters.

2 Select a master

Editing masters

The illustration shown here is a Title master. You can use the same techniques in any master.

| Click in a text entry, then apply any appropriate formatting enhancements

For how to insert pictures into master slides, see Chapter 6.

For how to work with headers/ footers, see pages 84–86.

To format text within masters, use the techniques discussed on pages 49–51.

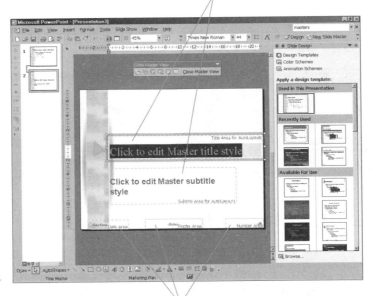

2 Click in a specialised text box, then apply any appropriate formatting enhancements

Adding new masters

PowerPoint 2002 is set up to permit multiple masters. If you don't want this, choose Tools, Options. In the Options dialog, select the Edit tab. Tick Multiple Masters in the Disable new features section. Click OK.

You can replace existing masters with new ones from design templates. Alternatively, you can simply add new ones.

Replacing/inserting new masters

1 Pull down the View menu and click Master, Slide Master

2 Optional – to replace specific masters, select one or more

Re step 3 – choose Replace All Designs or Replace Selected Designs for a substitution, or Add Design for a new addition.

Masters come in pairs: the Slide and the Title Master:

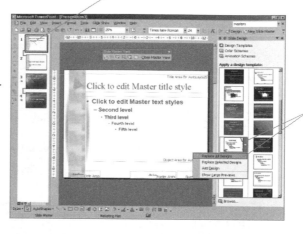

3 Right-click a design then specify how it should be applied

Slide master

5

6

Title master

PowerPoint makes it clear they're linked by attaching a link symbol (see on the left of the illustration above).

To make changes to either master, select it.

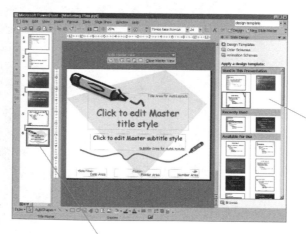

Design templates used in the current slide show display in the Used in This Presentation section of the Task Pane

4 Here, an additional master pair has been inserted

Master housekeeping

You can perform various actions on masters.

Renaming masters

To duplicate a master, carry out step 1 — however, left-click one master (or Ctrl+click multiple masters) instead. Pull down the Insert menu and select Duplicate Slide Master.

On the left of the Master, right-click a master thumbnail (or first select multiple thumbnails then right-click one)

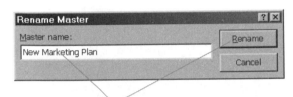

3 Enter a new name and click Rename

2 In the menu, click Rename

Protecting masters

When you protect a master, PowerPoint inserts this symbol to the left of its thumbnail:

To prevent a master from being automatically deleted (e.g. when all associated slides are deleted), follow step 1 above

2 In the menu, click Preserve Master

Deleting masters

Follow step 1 above

2 In the menu, click Delete Master – deletion is immediate (but can be undone, if necessary)

Within any master, you can restore elements/placeholders you've previously deleted.

You can also use Undo to restore elements.

Restoring masters

Pull down the Format menu and do one of the following:

- click Master Layout (re. Slide and Title masters)
- click Handout Master Layout (re. Handout masters), or;
- click Notes Master Layout (re. Notes masters)

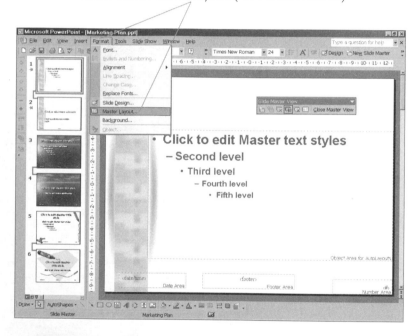

2 Tick the deleted element(s) and confirm

Applying colour schemes

Any PowerPoint 2002 presentation automatically has various colour schemes available to it (they're contained in the design template associated with the slide show). Design templates can have up to 16 colour schemes.

Applying a new colour scheme is a quick and effective way to give a presentation a new and consistent look. Making slight but telling changes to existing schemes is also useful. For example, you might want to adapt a presentation's colours to fit a specific show or event... PowerPoint 2002 lets you do this very easily and conveniently.

Another plus is the fact that when you apply colours independently of colour schemes (e.g. when you recolour text via the Font dialog), the new colours are automatically made available in colour dialogs in a way which makes it clear they're distinct from colour scheme colours (see the tip). This means it's very easy to maintain colour consistency.

In the example below, a non-standard colour has been applied to text. As a result, launching the Color fly-out in the Font dialog produces this result:

The 8 colour scheme colours

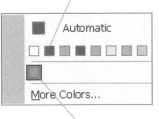

The new colour

Imposing a colour scheme

If you want to restrict the colour scheme to one or more slides, first do one of the following:

- In Normal view, go to the slide whose colour scheme you want to replace

- In Slide Sorter or Thumbnail view, select one or more slides

Now pull down the Format menu and carry out the following:

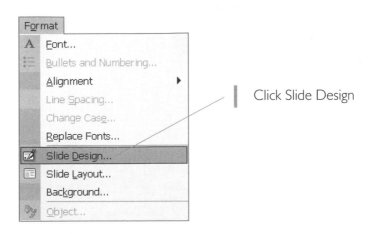

Click Slide Design

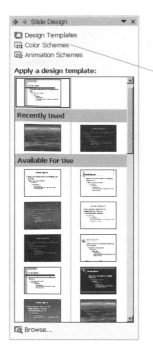

To modify colours for a notes page, choose View, Notes Page before you carry out the procedures here.

(To change all notes pages in a presentation, first choose View, Master, Notes Master.)

2 Click Color Schemes

Some design templates have more colour schemes associated with them than others.

When you change the colours in a colour scheme, PowerPoint creates a new scheme and adds it to the Color Schemes version of the Slide Design Task Pane.

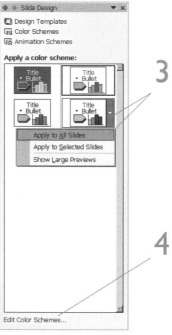

3 Click on the right of a colour scheme, then specify how it should be applied

4 Click here to edit the colour scheme selected in step 3 (then see the facing page)

Changing colours in a scheme

You can change individual colours within a colour scheme. When you do this, all associated slide objects are automatically updated.

Amending a scheme colour

If you want to restrict the change to one or more slides, first do one of the following:

- In Normal view, go to the slide whose colour scheme you want to replace

- In Slide Sorter or Thumbnail view, select multiple slides

Now do the following:

1 Follow steps 1–2 on pages 77–78. Select a scheme. Carry out step 4

Colours in colour schemes resemble word processor graphics styles.

To see what your slides would look like after the proposed changes, click Preview.

To delete a colour scheme, select the Standard tab in step 2. Select a scheme and click Delete Scheme. Select Apply.
(You can't delete a slide show's one remaining colour scheme.)

To ensure that the colour changes you've made are saved with the slide show, click the Add as Standard Scheme button:

Repeat steps 3-6 for as many colours as you want to change.

Re step 5 – insert new Red, Green and Blue values, as appropriate.

2 Select Custom

3 Select a slide component, then Change Color

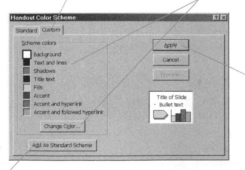

7 Click Apply

4 Click the Custom tab

6 Click OK

5 Drag this to a new location, or type in new values here:

Format Painter

PowerPoint 2002 offers a useful shortcut (Format Painter) which enables you to copy a colour scheme:

- from one slide to another

- from one slide to multiple slides

Copying colour schemes within a single slide show

Click the slide whose colour scheme you want to copy

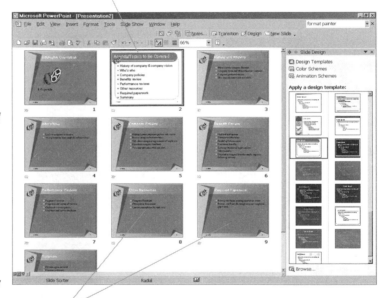

Here, Format Painter is being used in Slide Sorter view. However, you can also carry out steps 1 and 3 with Thumbnail view.

If the Standard toolbar isn't currently on-screen, pull down the View menu and click Toolbars, Standard.

If you double-clicked the Format Painter icon, press Esc when you've finished copying the colour scheme.

3 Click the slide(s) you want to apply the colour scheme to

2 In the Standard toolbar, click here for 1 copy or double-click for multiple copies

You can also use Format Painter to copy formatting between objects (e.g. pictures/clip art).

You can also use Format Painter to copy colour schemes between open presentations.

Copying colour schemes between slide shows

1 With both presentations open in Normal view, pull down the Window menu and click Arrange All

2 Carry out step 3 below. In step 4, single-click for one copy or double-click for multiple copies (and see the HOT TIP):

4 Click or double-click the Format Painter icon in the Standard toolbar:

3 Click the icon representing the slide whose scheme you want to copy

To copy the formatting to more than one slide, double-click in step 4. In step 5, click as many icons as required. When you've finished, press Esc.

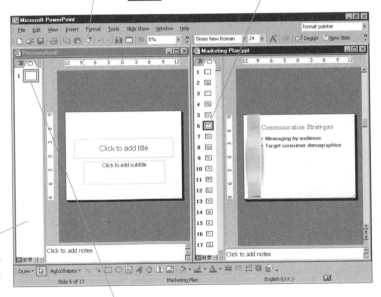

To use Format Painter to copy colour schemes between slide shows, ensure the Thumbnail tab is enabled in Outline view.

5 Click the icon representing the slide you want to format

Applying design templates

The *AutoContent wizard uses a specialised form of design template called the content template. (See the DON'T FORGET tip on page 36.)*

When you apply a new design template to a presentation, you impose a potent combination of masters and colour schemes. For this reason, designs often represent the best and most convenient way to give presentations an effective and consistent appearance.

Imposing a design

The Slide Design Task Pane defaults to the folder which holds PowerPoint 2002 templates. If you want to use templates stored in a different drive/folder combination, select Browse at the base of the Task Pane and select it in the Apply Design Template dialog.

1 If you want to restrict the change to one or more slides, first do one of the following:

- In Normal view, go to the slide you want to apply the new design template to

- In Slide Sorter or Thumbnail view, select multiple slides

2 Pull down the Format menu and click Slide Design

You can also use slide shows, HTML files or web archives as the basis for a design.

Launch the Apply Design Template dialog (see the above tip.) In the dialog, click in the Files of type: field and select the appropriate format. Locate then double-click the file you want to use.

3 Click on the right of a design template

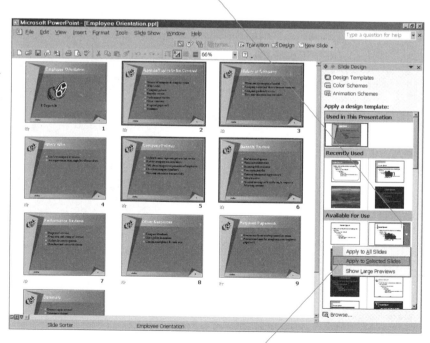

To have design templates display more clearly, right-click one in the Task Pane. In the menu, select Show Large Previews.

4 Specify the extent of the change

Applying new backgrounds

You can also apply new backgrounds to slides, as a separate action.

Imposing a background

1 If you want to restrict the change to one or more slides, first do one of the following:

- In Normal view, go to the slide you want to apply the new design template to

- In Slide Sorter or Thumbnail view, select multiple slides

2 Pull down the Format menu and click Background

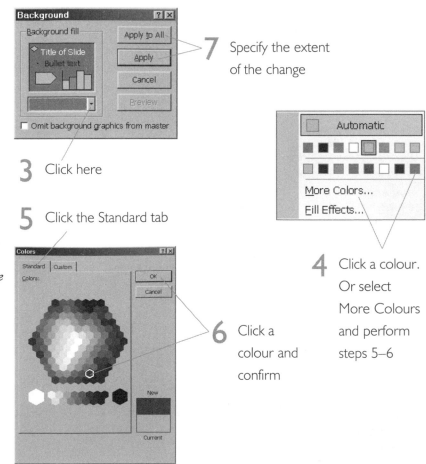

7 Specify the extent of the change

3 Click here

5 Click the Standard tab

You can apply fill effects (gradients, textures and patterns) to backgrounds. You can also apply other pictures as fills.
Follow steps 1–3 then select Fill Effects. In the Fill Effects dialog, select a tab (e.g. Gradient). Complete the rest of the dialog and click OK.

4 Click a colour. Or select More Colours and perform steps 5–6

6 Click a colour and confirm

Working with headers/footers

Headers are text elements which appear at the top of handouts or notes (see page 86); footers are elements which appear at the base of slides, handouts or notes.

Typically, you'll use headers and footers to display:

- the date and time of the presentation

- the slide or page number

- information specific to the current presentation

Once you've inserted information in headers and/or footers, you can change their appearance or position.

Using footers in slides

If you want to restrict your amendments to one or more slides, first do one of the following:

- In Normal view, go to the slide whose footer you want to change

- In Slide Sorter or Thumbnail view, select multiple slides

Now pull down the View menu and do the following:

You don't have to use headers and footers in your slide shows. For instance, it might be helpful to disable them in slides but leave them in force in notes and handouts.

To move or reformat header and footer elements, launch the appropriate master. Select the element(s). Then do either or both of the following:

- *drag them to a new location*

- *apply new formatting characteristics (using the procedures discussed on pages 49–51)*

To add the date/time or slide number anywhere on a slide, click inside the relevant text placeholder or text box. Choose Insert, Slide Number or Insert, Date and Time.

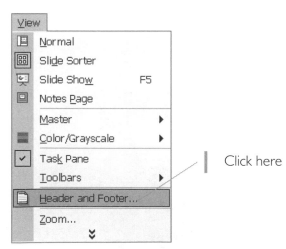

Click here

2 Carry out step 3 below then do the following as appropriate:

- if you don't want the date and time to display automatically in the footer area, follow step 4

- if you want to customise how the date and time display, omit step 4; follow step 5 instead

- if you want the slide number to display in the footer, perform step 6

- to insert specific slide information in the footer, carry out step 7

- finally, perform step 8 to apply the header/footer changes to all slides within the presentation. Alternatively, to apply them only to slides pre-selected before step 1, carry out step 9

To amend the number at which slide numbering begins, choose File, Page Setup. In the Number slides from: field, type in a new start point. Click OK.

Re step 4 – tick here: instead if you want the current date and time to be inserted automatically.

To remove footers from title slides, tick Don't show on title slide.
To disable footers in all other slides, untick the fields flagged by steps 4–7.

3 Ensure the Slide tab is active

4 Deselect Date and time

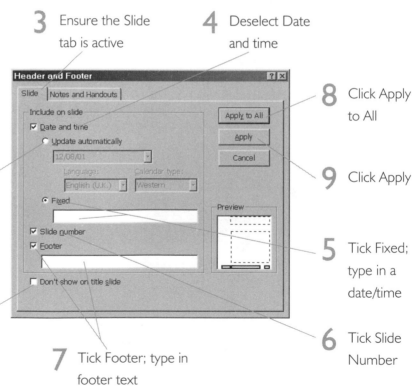

8 Click Apply to All

9 Click Apply

5 Tick Fixed; type in a date/time

6 Tick Slide Number

7 Tick Footer; type in footer text

Using headers/footers in notes and handouts

1 Follow step 1 on page 84

2 Carry out step 3 below then do the following as appropriate:

- if you don't want the date and time to display automatically in the footer area, follow step 4
- if you want to customise how the date and time display, omit step 4; follow step 5 instead
- if you want the page number to display, perform step 6
- to insert specific slide information in the footer, carry out step 7
- finally, perform step 8 to apply the header/footer changes to all slides within the active presentation

 To disable headers and footers in all handouts and notes, untick the fields flagged by steps 4-7.

 Re step 5 – click here: instead if you want the current date and time to be inserted automatically.

 If you want a specific header, tick Header and type it in the Header field.

3 Ensure the Notes and Handouts tab is active

4 Deselect Date and time

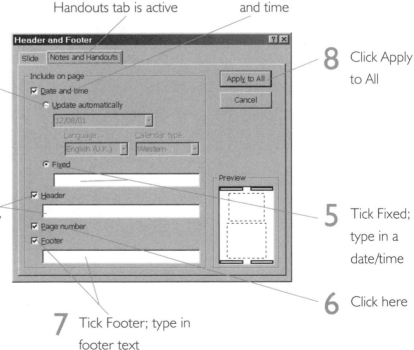

8 Click Apply to All

5 Tick Fixed; type in a date/time

6 Click here

7 Tick Footer; type in footer text

Working with objects

In this chapter, you'll create and insert 'objects' (simple or complex graphics) in order to make your presentations even more visually effective. You'll create lines, arrows, curves, rectangles/squares and ellipses/circles, then create AutoShapes (extraordinarily flexible graphics which are very easy to use) including special lines which you can attach to objects. You'll go on to reformat your objects (especially AutoShapes) to customise them for use in your slides – you'll rotate them, apply fills/shadows and convert them to 3D. Finally, you'll insert WordArt text objects and save your objects to disk.

Covers

Chapter Four

Objects – an overview

You can use the following method to edit inserted objects (in addition to the techniques discussed on pages 97–101).

Double-click any object to produce the Format AutoShape dialog. Activate the appropriate tab, then make the necessary amendments. For example, to amend the object's size, click the Size tab and enter new settings in the Height/Width fields (in either the Size and rotate or the Scale sections).

Finally, click OK.

You can add a variety of objects to your presentations:

- lines

- arrowed lines

- simple shapes (squares/rectangles and circles/ellipses)

- curves and freeform curve/line combinations

- a wide assortment of flexible shapes (known as AutoShapes) including 'sticky' lines known as connectors

The judicious inclusion of objects in your slide shows makes them more visual and can considerably enhance their effect.

AutoShapes are ready-made shapes you can define and manipulate with just a few mouse clicks. They're readily adjustable, and fall into several categories. These include:

Action Buttons	*Stars and Banners*
Basic Shapes	*Callouts*

When you've inserted objects, you can manipulate them in several ways. You can:

- move them

- resize them

- rotate/flip them

- apply a colour/fill

- apply a shadow

- make them 3D

- (in the case of *complex* AutoShapes – see the DON'T FORGET tip on page 89) convert them into other shapes

All inserted objects can also be resized/ moved with the use of standard Windows mouse techniques.

Creating lines

Technically, all objects you insert in PowerPoint 2002 are AutoShapes.

However, this book makes a functional distinction between simple objects (lines, curves etc.) and the more complex AutoShapes discussed on pages 97–101.

PowerPoint 2002 lets you create:

* straight lines

* single-arrowed lines

* double-arrowed lines

* curved lines (see pages 93–94)

* freeform lines (see pages 95–96)

Creating a straight line

First, ensure you're using Normal or Notes Pages view. Refer to the Drawing toolbar and do the following:

You can also create lines which 'stick' to the shapes they contact.

Follow step 1 on page 97. In step 2, select Connectors. In 3, click a connector. Now move the pointer over the object you want to attach the connector to. Click a connection site (a blue circle). Find another site in a second object and click it.

(Attached connectors show as red circles, unattached ones as green circles.)

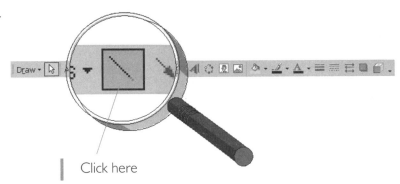

Click here

2 Click where you want the line to begin and drag to define the line

Re step 2 – to constrain the new line to 15° increments, hold down one Shift key as you define it.

Re step 2 – to define the line outwards (to the left and right) from the starting point, hold down Ctrl as you drag.

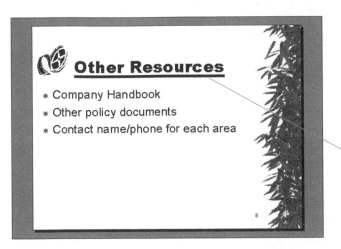

An inserted line

To create a double-arrowed line, click *AutoShapes* in the *Drawing* toolbar. Select *Lines* and then this icon:

Drag to define the line.

Re step 2 – to constrain the new line to 15° increments, hold down one Shift key as you define it.

Re step 2 – to define the line outwards (to the left and right) from the starting point, hold down Ctrl as you drag.

The lines in these examples have been thickened. To thicken a line (or other object), select it. Refer to the *Drawing* toolbar and click this icon:

In the graphic list, select a line weight. (Or click *More Lines* and use the *Colors and Lines* section of the *Format AutoShape* dialog to customise a line.)

Creating a single-arrowed line

First, ensure you're using Normal or Notes Pages view. Refer to the Drawing toolbar and do the following:

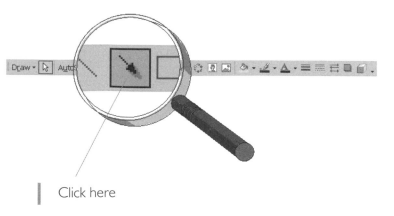

Click here

2 Click where you want the arrowed line to begin and drag to define the line

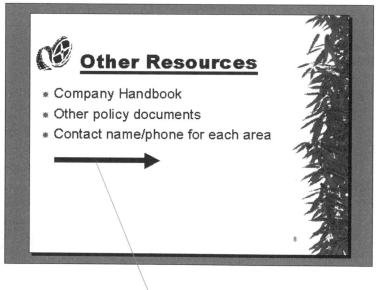

The inserted line

Creating rectangles

You can use another route to create a rectangle/ square.

Follow step 1 then click in your slide where you want the rectangle/square to begin. PowerPoint 2002 inserts the following (with or without the fill):

Ensure this prototype object is selected then resize it appropriately (for how to do this, see 'Resizing AutoShapes' on page 98).

To create a square, hold down Shift as you drag.

To apply fills to objects, follow the techniques described on page 99.

Drawing a rectangle

First, ensure you're using Normal or Notes Pages view. Refer to the Drawing toolbar and do the following:

1 Click here

2 Place the mouse pointer where you want one corner of the rectangle to begin

3 Click and hold down the left mouse button, then drag to create the rectangle

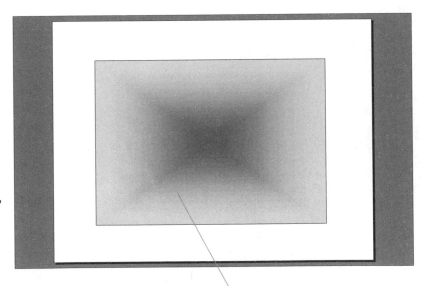

An inserted rectangle, plus a gradient fill

Creating ellipses

You can use another route to create an ellipse/circle. Follow step 1 above. Then click in your slide where you want the object to begin. PowerPoint 2002 inserts the following (with or without the fill):

Ensure this prototype ellipse/circle is selected then resize it appropriately (for how to do this, see 'Resizing AutoShapes' on page 98, or the HOT TIP on page 88).

To create a circle, hold down Shift as you drag.

To apply fills to objects, follow the techniques described on page 99.

Drawing an ellipse

First, ensure you're using Normal or Notes Pages view. Refer to the Drawing toolbar and do the following:

| Click here

2 Place the mouse pointer where you want one corner of the ellipse to begin

3 Click and hold down the left mouse button then drag to create the ellipse

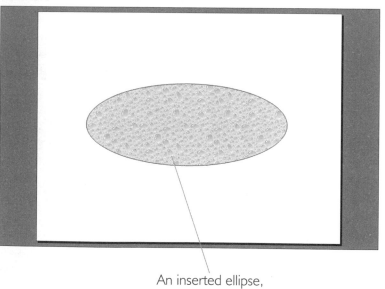

An inserted ellipse,
plus a texture fill

Creating Bézier curves

PowerPoint 2002 lets you create three types of curves:

Bezier	Great control and accuracy – pages 93–94
Freeform	Freehand curve/line combinations without jagged edges – page 95
Scribble	A lifelike imitation of freehand drawing – page 96

Defining Bézier curves

If you need to create curves, you'll normally use this technique. In effect, you tell PowerPoint where 2 or more points should be placed and it creates the appropriate curve(s) between them.

1 Ensure you're using Normal or Notes Pages view. Refer to the Drawing toolbar and click AutoShapes. Select Lines. Click this icon:

2 Place the mouse pointer where you want the curve to begin

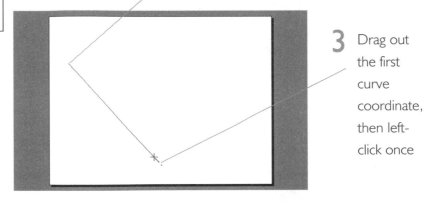

3 Drag out the first curve coordinate, then left-click once

4 Move the pointer to complete the 1st curve then left-click once

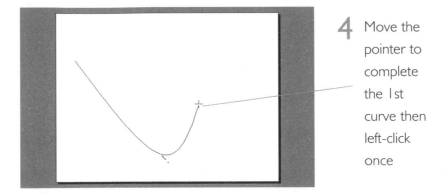

5 Optional – move the mouse pointer to define another curve, then left-click

Re step 7 – use a different procedure if you want to produce a closed shape e.g.

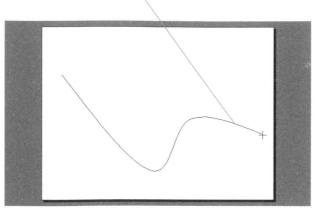

Simply left-click once near the curve start point.

6 Repeat step 5 as often as required

7 When you've finished defining curves, double-click once

A completed Bézier curve:

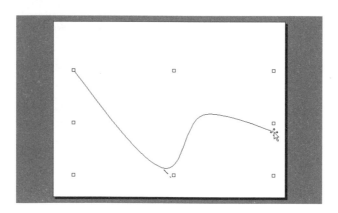

Creating freeform curves/lines

Using the Freeform tool

Use the Freeform tool to create objects with both curved and straight components.

First, ensure you're using Normal or Notes Pages view. Refer to the Drawing toolbar and do the following:

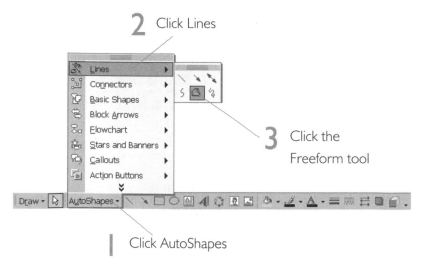

2 Click Lines

3 Click the Freeform tool

1 Click AutoShapes

You should perform step 5 OR 6, as appropriate. (Do so as often as required.)

4 Place the mouse pointer where you want the object to begin

5 Click and hold down the left mouse button, then drag to create a freehand shape, OR:

Re step 7 – use a different procedure if you want to produce a closed shape e.g.

6 Left-click, then move the mouse pointer and left-click again, to create a straight line

7 When you've finished drawing, double-click once

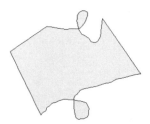

Simply left-click once near the object start point.

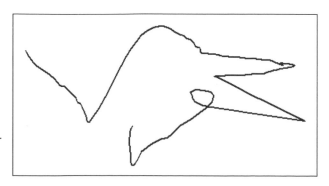

A freeform curve/line combination

Creating curves with Scribble

Use the Scribble tool to create objects which look as if they were drawn with a pen.

Using the Scribble tool

First, ensure you're using Normal or Notes Pages view. Refer to the Drawing toolbar and do the following:

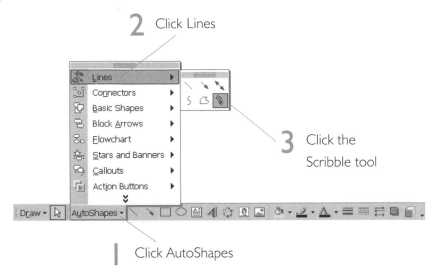

2 Click Lines

3 Click the Scribble tool

1 Click AutoShapes

Re step 5 – use a different procedure if you want to produce a closed shape e.g.

4 Place the mouse pointer where you want your curve to begin

5 Click and hold down the left mouse button, then drag out the curve

Simply left-click once near the object start point.

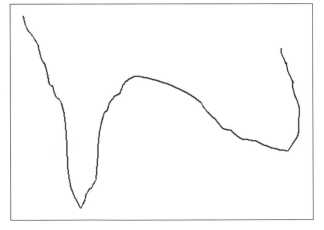

A curve created with Scribble

Creating AutoShapes

You can easily add text to inserted AutoShapes. Right-click the AutoShape. In the menu, click Add Text. The insertion point appears inside the figure; type in the text. Click outside the AutoShape.

AutoShapes represent an extraordinarily flexible and easy-to-use way to insert a wide variety of shapes into your presentations. Once inserted, they can be:

- resized

- rotated/flipped

- coloured/filled

- converted into other shapes

Inserting an AutoShape

You can have an AutoShape (or text box) resize to fit the text it contains.

 Double-click the AutoShape or text box frame. In the dialog, select the Text Box tab and tick Resize AutoShape to fit text. Click OK.

First, ensure you're using Normal or Notes Pages view. Refer to the Drawing toolbar and do the following:

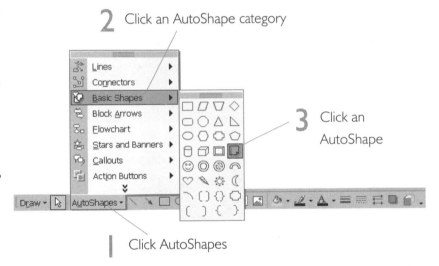

2 Click an AutoShape category

3 Click an AutoShape

Click AutoShapes

Changes you make to an AutoShape also affect any inserted text.

4 Place the mouse pointer where you want your AutoShape to begin

You can use a shortcut to insert AutoShapes. Follow steps 1-3, then simply click where you want the AutoShape inserted. Now resize it appropriately – see page 98.

5 Click and hold down the left mouse button, then drag out the shape

Resizing/rotating AutoShapes

To rotate in 90° stages, don't follow steps 1 or 2. Instead, click the Draw button. In the menu, click Rotate or Flip. In the sub-menu, click Rotate Left or Rotate Right.

Many of the techniques discussed on this and later pages in this chapter can be applied to text boxes, too.

Use any of the procedures on this and the facing page to adjust existing fills.

You can also use another technique to rotate an AutoShapes. Select it then do the following:

Drag here

Resizing AutoShapes

Select the AutoShape. Now do the following:

Drag any handle inwards or outwards

Rotating AutoShapes

Select the AutoShape. Now refer to the Drawing toolbar and do the following:

1 Click Draw. In the menu, select Rotate or Flip, Free Rotate

2 Place the mouse pointer over one of the handles

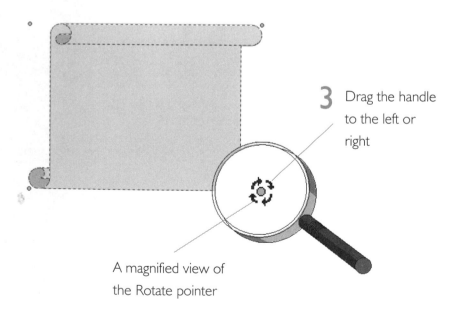

3 Drag the handle to the left or right

A magnified view of the Rotate pointer

Filling AutoShapes

Most AutoShapes have a special yellow handle:

Magnified view of AutoShape handle

Dragging on this changes the AutoShape's shape (but not its size).

Re step 3 – to apply a special fill, click Fill Effects instead. Complete the Fill Effects dialog. For example, to apply a gradient, select the Gradient tab and enter the relevant parameters. Or, to use a picture as a fill, select the Picture tab. Click the Select Picture button. Now use the Select Picture dialog to locate and double-click the relevant image.

Finally, click OK.

Re step 4 – if you want to define your own colour, click the Custom tab instead. Click a colour in the Colors: box. Drag the slider on the right to adjust the brightness. Finally, omit step 5; instead, click OK.

Colouring AutoShapes

In Normal or Notes Pages view, select the AutoShape. Refer to the Drawing toolbar, then carry out step 1. If the available colours are suitable, perform step 2. If not, carry out steps 3–5 instead:

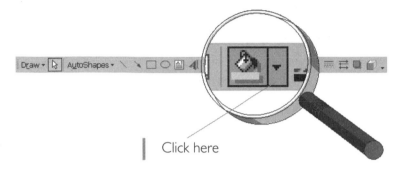

Click here

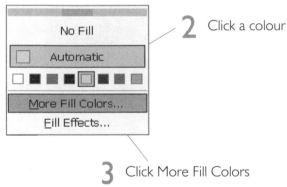

2 Click a colour

3 Click More Fill Colors

4 Activate the Standard tab

5 Double-click a colour

Shadowing AutoShapes

In Normal or Notes Pages view, select the relevant AutoShape. Refer to the Drawing toolbar and do the following:

You can use these techniques (and those on the facing page) with any drawing object created in PowerPoint 2002.

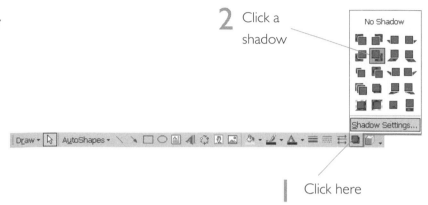

2 Click a shadow

Click here

Fine-tuning shadows

It's often a good idea to 'tweak' the shadow PowerPoint gives you, to make it more effective.

1 Select the AutoShape. Perform step 1 above. In 2, select Shadow Settings

Re step 2 – the flagged buttons move the shadow up, down, left and right.

2 Click one of these (as often as required) to vary the shadow position

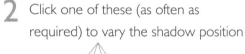

Shadow Color button

To vary the shadow colour, click on the right of the Shadow Color button in the toolbar. Select a colour. Alternatively, select More Shadow Colors and complete the Colors dialog (e.g. activate the Standard tab and double-click a colour) then click OK.

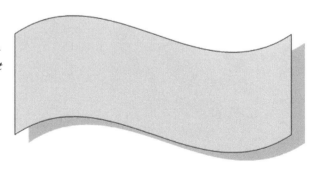

This object's shadow has been accentuated to the right and down

Converting AutoShapes

To vary the 3D colour, select the object. Follow step 1. In the pop-up 3D list, click the 3-D Settings button. The 3-D Settings toolbar launches. Do the following:

Making AutoShapes 3D

In Normal or Notes Pages view, select the AutoShape. Refer to the Drawing toolbar and do the following:

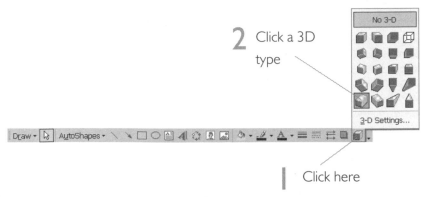

2 Click a 3D type

Click here

Click here; in the drop-down list, click a colour

Alternatively, click More 3-D Colors in the list, then carry out steps 4–5 on page 99.)

Converting AutoShapes from one type to another

In Normal or Notes Pages view, select the AutoShape. Refer to the Drawing toolbar and do the following:

To control the tilt of a 3D object, select it. Then click any of these icons (as often as required) in the 3-D Settings toolbar:

2 Click Change AutoShape

4 Click a new AutoShape

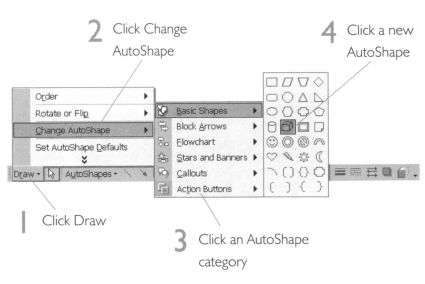

Click Draw

3 Click an AutoShape category

Up and Down tilt

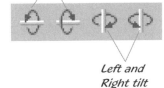

Left and Right tilt

Using WordArt

In Normal or Notes Page view, you can embellish your slides with WordArt objects. These are text objects with professional-quality, ready-made formatting attributes. WordArt text can add a lot of pizazz to slides.

Adding a WordArt object

You can save any AutoShape or WordArt object to disk. Right-click it and choose Save as Picture in the menu. In the Save As Picture dialog, select an output format (choose Windows Metafile... if you want to re-edit the picture). Name the picture and select an output drive/folder. Finally, click Save.

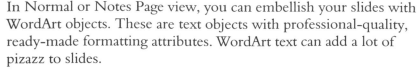

Click here in the Drawing toolbar

To change a WordArt object's textual content, double-click it. In the Edit WordArt Text dialog, overwrite the selected text and click OK.

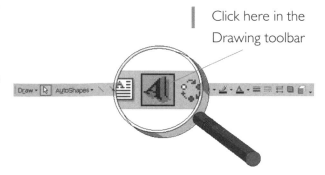

2 Double-click a style

Before step 3, set the relevant formatting options (e.g. specify a font and type size):

For an example of WordArt in action, see page 70.

Re step 3 – press Enter to insert a paragraph return.

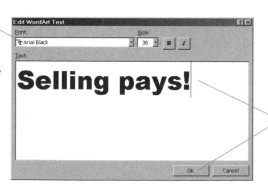

3 Type in the text you want the style applied to and confirm

Using charts

Charts dramatically improve slide impact. In this chapter, you'll learn about chart terminology and create and insert new charts. You can do this from within PowerPoint 2002 itself (and other programs) with the help of the Datasheet, an inbuilt mini-spreadsheet – you'll learn how to select data, add/hide various components and add new cells. Alternatively, you'll create charts seamlessly from imported data in a variety of external formats.

Once you've created charts, you'll allocate a new chart type (a technique you can also use to create combination charts), set up a default type and create your own. Finally, you'll add text boxes and reformat the various chart components (including adding complex fills and borders).

Covers

Chapter Five

Charts – an overview

PowerPoint 2002 makes it easy to insert charts into your presentations. You can do this in two ways:

- by double-clicking chart placeholders (if the slide you're inserting the chart into has had the appropriate layout applied to it)

- by using a menu route

When you create or work with charts in PowerPoint 2002, you're actually running a separate program: Microsoft Graph.
Graph runs seamlessly within the PowerPoint 2002 environment (but note that, unlike PowerPoint itself, its menus are not personalised i.e. entries aren't promoted or demoted according to frequency of use).

When you insert a chart, the data on which it's based is displayed in a special window called the Datasheet. The Datasheet can be regarded as a mini version of a typical spreadsheet, and contains sample data which you can easily amend.

Once you've inserted a chart, you can:

- edit the data

- reformat the Datasheet

- import data from a variety of external sources, including Microsoft Excel files

- apply a new chart type/sub-type

- reformat chart objects

You can also use Graph to insert charts into other programs (e.g. Word 2002).
In the program, pull down the Insert menu and click Object (this command sometimes varies with the program concerned). Select the Create New tab and double-click Microsoft Graph Chart. Now customise/edit it in the usual way.

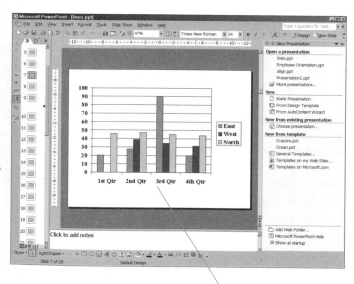

An inserted chart, with sample data

Chart components

PowerPoint 2002 offers 14 overall chart types. There are also numerous sub-types (variants on a theme). In addition, PowerPoint 2002 charts are very customisable: they can contain a wide variety of features/components. The illustration below shows the main ones:

Most charts do not contain all of these elements (they would simply become too cluttered); they're shown here for illustration purposes.

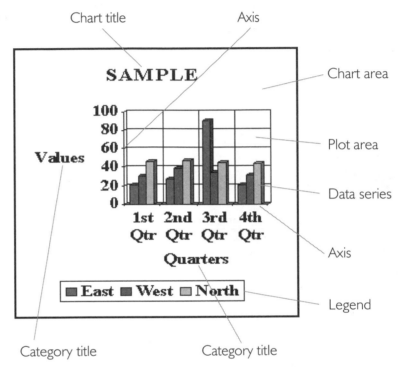

Terminology...

A data series is a group of related values taken from a Datasheet row (horizontal) or column (vertical). In this chart, there are three: East, West and North. (For more information on the use of the Datasheet, see pages 107–109.)

The distinctions listed here between the X, Y and Z axes are sometimes blurred.

Axes are lines which border the chart area; chart values are measured against axes. In most charts, the Y (Value) axis is vertical, while the X (Category) axis is horizontal.

Some charts also have a Z (Time) axis which allows values to be related to time.

Inserting charts

The placeholder route

In Normal view, display the slide into which you want to insert the chart. Carry out the following steps:

Re step 1 – some slide layouts have a different placeholder. Do the following:

Click here

Re step 2 – for how to complete the Datasheet, see page 107.

To create a chart via a menu route, pull down the Insert menu and click Chart. Now complete the Datasheet.

To insert new blank cells into the Datasheet, select a range equal to the number you want to insert. Choose Insert, Cells.

To hide axes in a chart, select it. Pull down the Chart menu and click Chart Options. In the dialog, select the Axes tab and untick the relevant entries. Click OK.

Double-click the Chart placeholder

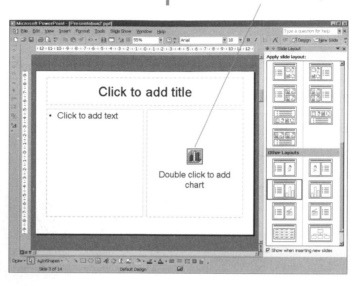

2 Complete the Datasheet, then click anywhere in the slide

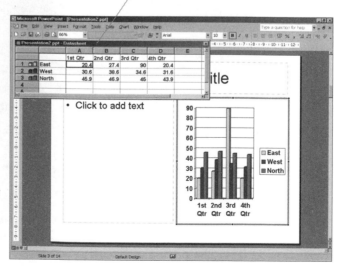

Editing chart data

To add a legend to a chart, select it. Pull down the Chart menu and click Chart Options. In the dialog, select the Legend tab and tick Show legend. Select a placement (e.g. Bottom) and click OK.

(To hide an existing legend, untick Show legend).

After you've created a chart, and irrespective of the way you created it, you have to revise the data on which it's based. PowerPoint 2002 makes this process easy and convenient.

Amending data

Right-click over the chart you want to amend. Do the following:

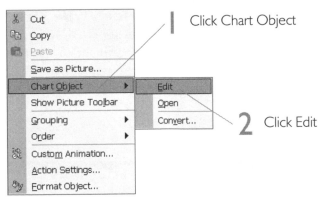

1 Click Chart Object

2 Click Edit

To add a chart title and/or axis titles to a chart, select it. Pull down the Chart menu and click Chart Options. In the dialog, select the Titles tab and type in the relevant titles. Click OK.

PowerPoint 2002 launches the Datasheet. Perform any of steps 3–5, then carry out step 6:

To add gridlines to a chart, select it. Choose Chart, Chart Options. In the dialog, select the Gridlines tab and tick the relevant entries. Click OK.

3 Amend the axis titles

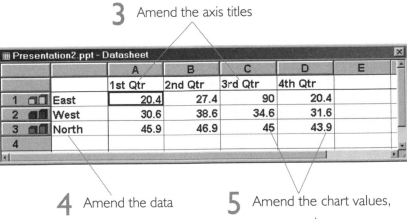

Cells are formed where rows and columns intersect.

4 Amend the data series titles

5 Amend the chart values, as appropriate

If you want to hide the Datasheet while leaving the chart active, pull down the View menu and click Datasheet.

(Repeat to show the Datasheet again.)

6 When you've finished, click outside the Datasheet

Reformatting the Datasheet

Formatting changes you make to the Datasheet have no effect on the way your data is represented in the associated chart, but they can make it easier to edit your data effectively.

To a limited extent, you can customise how the Datasheet presents information. You can:

- change the typeface/type size

- specify how numbers display (e.g. you can set the number of decimal points)

Applying a typeface/type size

Double-click the relevant chart. If the Datasheet isn't visible, pull down the View menu and click Datasheet. Pull down the Format menu and click Font. Carry out step 1 and/or 2 below, as appropriate. Finally, perform step 3:

Click a font

You can also embolden and/ or italicise text. Click one of the options here:

before you carry out step 3.

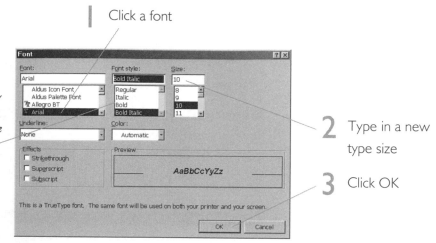

2 Type in a new type size

3 Click OK

The end result:

In all graph types apart from XY (Scatter) and Bubble (where the first row or column holds data), the initial row and column in the Datasheet contain identifying text.

Column headings

		A	B	C	D	E
		1st Qtr	2nd Qtr	3rd Qtr	4th Qtr	
1	East	20.4	27.4	90	20.4	
2	West	30.6	38.6	34.6	31.6	
3	North	45.9	46.9	45	43.9	
4						

Presentation2.ppt - Datasheet

The font has been italicised

Row headings

...cont'd

To select multiple cells, first click the cell which forms the upper-left boundary of the cells you want to select. Hold down the mouse button and drag over the remaining cells. Release the mouse button.

To select a single cell, simply click in it.

To select an entire row in the Datasheet, click its row heading; to select a whole column, click its column heading (see the facing page).

To select all cells, click the Select All button – see below:

Select All button

Applying a number format

Double-click the relevant chart. (If the Datasheet isn't visible, pull down the View menu and click Datasheet.) Select the cells you want to amend, then pull down the Format menu and carry out step 1 below. Perform step 2 and/or 3, as appropriate. Finally, perform step 4:

1 Click Number

2 Click a number format

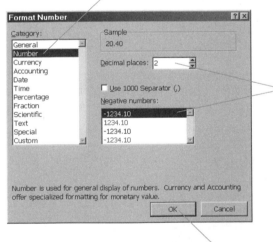

3 Complete the relevant options (they depend on the format chosen in step 2)

4 Click here

The end result:

		A	B	C	D	E
		1st Qtr	2nd Qtr	3rd Qtr	4th Qtr	
1	East	20	27	90	20	
2	West	31	39	35	32	
3	North	46	47	45	44	
4						

With 0 decimal places

Importing data from Excel

Most database and spreadsheet programs readily export data as text files (data files which lack formatting codes).

There are different types. For example, units of data can be differentiated ('delimited') by:

* *commas (probably the most common)*

* *tabs*

* *spaces*

You can have PowerPoint 2002 create charts from third-party data. You can import:

* Microsoft Excel files

* Lotus 1-2-3 files

* text files, also known as 'delimited' or CSV (Comma Separated Value) files

Importing Excel data

Within Normal view, go to the slide in which you want the new chart created. Pull down the Insert menu and click Chart; PowerPoint 2002 inserts a new chart with sample data and launches the Datasheet. If you want the inserted data to begin in any cell other than the upper left, click it. Pull down the Edit menu and click Import File. Now carry out the following:

Re step 2 – you can also carry out one of the following procedures:

* *Windows NT 4 and 98 users – use Network Neighborhood to import from a local network folder and Web Folders to import from a web/FTP folder*

* *Windows 2000 and Me users – use My Network Places to import from a local network folder or from a web/FTP folder*

Click any entry here for a useful shortcut. (For instance, to import data from a file on your Desktop, click Desktop...)

2 Click here. In the drop-down list, click the drive which hosts the Excel file

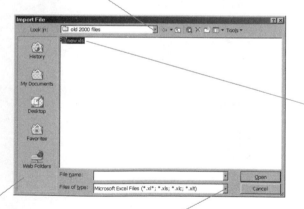

3 Double-click the file you want to import (you may have to double-click one or more folders first)

Click here; select Microsoft Excel Files... in the list

...cont'd

Re step 4 – data in Excel 2002 workbooks (files) is organised into individual worksheets. You can only select a worksheet with Excel 5.0 (or later) files.

(For more on Excel, see 'Excel 2002 in easy steps'.)

Re step 5 – type in the start and end cell addresses, separated by a colon.

For instance, to chart only cells H8 to K11, type:

H8:K11

PowerPoint 2002 now launches a special dialog. Carry out the following steps:

4 Select an Excel worksheet

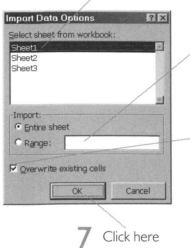

5 If you only want to import specific cells, type in the relevant range

6 Optional – deselect this if you don't want the contents of existing cells overwritten

7 Click here

Note that importing data is subject to the following restrictions:

- *maximum number or rows and columns – 4000 each*
- *maximum number of data series – 255*

You can also copy-and-paste information from other programs.

Select the data you want to copy. In the Datasheet, click the cell where you want the copied data to start. Press Ctrl+V.

PowerPoint 2002 now creates a new chart based on the imported data.

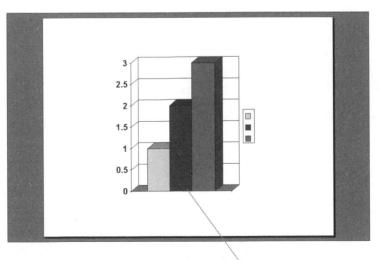

A (simple) inserted chart based on Excel data

Importing data from 1-2-3

Note that importing data is subject to the following restrictions:

- *maximum number or rows and columns – 4000 each*
- *maximum number of data series – 255*

Click any entry here for a useful shortcut. (For instance, to import data from a file on your Desktop, click Desktop...)

Re step 2 – you can also carry out one of the following procedures:

- *Windows NT 4 and 98 users – use Network Neighborhood to import from a local network folder and Web Folders to import from a web/FTP folder*
- *Windows 2000 and Me users – use My Network Places to import from a local network folder or from a web/FTP folder*

Importing 1-2-3 data

Within Normal view, go to the slide in which you want the new chart created. Pull down the Insert menu and click Chart; PowerPoint 2002 inserts a new chart with sample data and launches the Datasheet. If you want the inserted data to begin in any cell other than the upper left, click it. Pull down the Edit menu and click Import File. Now carry out the following:

2 Click here. In the drop-down list, click the drive which hosts the 1-2-3 file

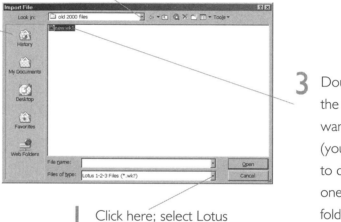

3 Double-click the file you want to import (you may have to double-click one or more folders first)

| Click here; select Lotus 1-2-3 Files... in the list

Caveat

In the case of Lotus 1-2-3 files, no further dialog launches. This means that you can only import the *whole* of a 1-2-3 file: you can't specify a cell range for inclusion within PowerPoint 2002.

If you only want to import a cell range, create a copy of the relevant 1-2-3 file and delete the unwanted cells within 1-2-3 itself. Then follow steps 1–3 to import the restricted file.

Importing data from text files

- *maximum number or rows and columns – 4000 each*

- *maximum number of data series – 255*

Click any entry here for a useful shortcut. (For instance, to import data from a file on your Desktop, click Desktop...)

Re step 2 – you can also carry out one of the following procedures:

- *Windows NT 4 and 98 users – use Network Neighborhood to import from a local network folder and Web Folders to import from a web/FTP folder*

- *Windows 2000 and Me users – use My Network Places to import from a local network folder or from a web/FTP folder*

Within Normal view, go to the slide in which you want the new chart created. Pull down the Insert menu and click Chart; PowerPoint 2002 inserts a new chart with sample data and launches the Datasheet. If you want the inserted data to begin in any cell other than the upper left, click it. Pull down the Edit menu and click Import File. Now carry out the following:

2 Click here. In the drop-down list, click the drive which hosts the text file

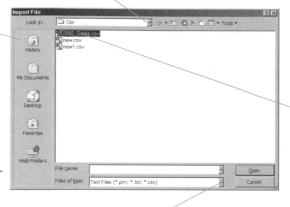

3 Double-click the file you want to import (you may have to double-click one or more folders first)

Click here; select Text Files... in the list

PowerPoint 2002 now launches a special wizard. It's worth going through this in some detail since importing text files can sometimes be tricky.

Complete each stage in line with the instructions on pages 114-115. However, you should note the following:

- PowerPoint 2002 auto-completes most of the settings in the wizard (and previews changes)

- only change these automatic settings if you're sure they're not suitable

Completing the Text Import Wizard

Carry out the following additional steps:

4 Optional – select another file type

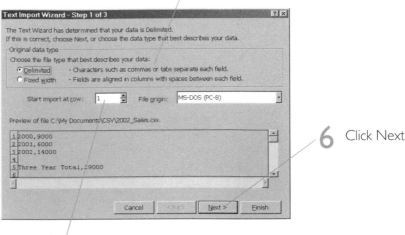

6 Click Next

Re step 7 – if you pick the incorrect delimiter, the data in the Preview section will look wrong e.g.

5 Optional – specify the row where the import begins

Wrong – the delimiters still show:

```
2000,9000
2001,6000
2002,14000

Three Year Total,29000
```

7 Optional – specify another delimiter

Right – they're invisible:

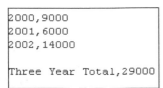

```
2000         9000
2001         6000
2002         14000

Three Year Total 29000
```

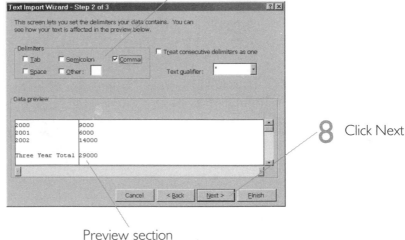

8 Click Next

Preview section

Carry out the following additional steps:

Repeat steps 9–10 for as many columns as you need to amend.

10 Optional – select a data format

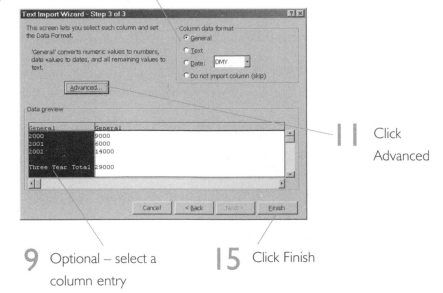

11 Click Advanced

Re step 12 – you need to select a separator which is identical to the decimal separator used in the original text file i.e. if the separator is a comma, choose the same.

(If in doubt, leave PowerPoint's choice unaltered.)

9 Optional – select a column entry

15 Click Finish

12 Click here; select a decimal separator

Re step 13 – you need to select a separator which is identical to the thousands separator used in the text file i.e. if the separator is a comma, choose the same.

(If in doubt, leave PowerPoint's choice unaltered.)

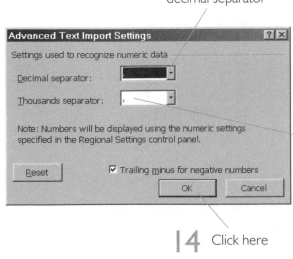

13 Click here; select a thousand separator

14 Click here

Applying a new chart type

Below are details of some of the main chart types:

Column	Compares items over time
Bar	As above, but less emphasis on time
Line	Best for displaying trends where the time element is equal
Area	Best for showing how parts relate to the whole, and for seeing the extent of changes
XY (Scatter)	Best for plotting several data series – used for scientific purposes
Pie	As Area, but only shows one data series

If you want, you can apply customised chart types. These are professionally designed formats which also incorporate:

- *colours*
- *patterns*
- *legends and other chart components*

To apply a custom type, don't follow step 2. Instead, activate the Custom Types tab. Then carry out steps 3 and 5–6 (omit 4 – custom charts don't have sub-types).

After you've inserted a chart, you can change the chart type. There are 14 overall chart types. Some of the most commonly used are described in the table on the left. All of the 14 types have a minimum of 2 sub-types associated with them. Often, the available sub-types include 3D alternatives.

You can combine chart types in what PowerPoint calls 'combination' charts. A common example is where bar and line chart types are combined so that the chart can display more than one information source. You combine types by applying more than one chart type to data series pre-selected before steps 1–6 below.

Changing chart types

Double-click the embedded chart in its host slide. Then do the following:

1 Pull down the Chart menu and click Chart Types

2 Ensure the Standard Types tab is active

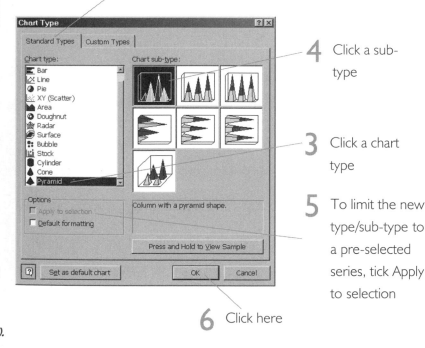

4 Click a sub-type

3 Click a chart type

5 To limit the new type/sub-type to a pre-selected series, tick Apply to selection

6 Click here

Colouring chart components

If you're recolouring text (e.g. the textual component of an axis, or a legend), follow step 1 but ignore steps 2–4. In the dialog, select the Font tab. Click the Color: box, then select a colour in the list. Click OK.

To specify a chart type as the default (i.e. PowerPoint uses it automatically when you create a new chart), follow steps 1–4 on the facing page. Now click Set as default chart and click OK.

You can create your own chart types (e.g. for distribution to colleagues).
Give the active chart the formatting you want. Select it. In step 2 on the facing page, select the Custom Types tab. Select User-defined, then click Add. Complete the Add Custom Chart Type dialog and click OK. The new type appears in the Chart type: field (as long as User-defined is selected).

After you've inserted a chart, you can easily vary the formatting. You can select specific chart objects and:

- apply a colour

- apply a texture/pattern as a fill

- change the line width/border style

- apply a new typeface/type size

Applying a colour

In Normal view, go to the slide which hosts the chart you want to amend. Double-click the chart. Now do the following:

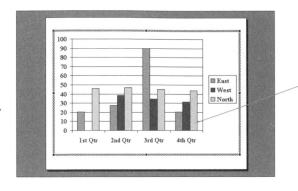

1 Double-click the component you want to recolour (here, a data series)

2 Ensure the Patterns tab is active

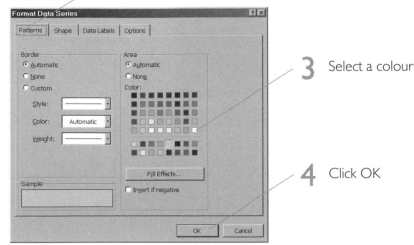

3 Select a colour

4 Click OK

Filling chart components

Applying a fill

In Normal view, go to the slide which hosts the chart you want to amend. Double-click the chart. Now double-click the chart component you want to fill. Carry out the following steps:

Re step 1 – select the other tabs (and complete the resultant dialog) to customise other chart aspects – but note that different graphs produce different tabs/ options.

Here, for example, select Shape and select a column shape. Or choose Data Labels and specify what the chart's data labels should contain (series/category names, or values).

1 Ensure the Patterns tab is active

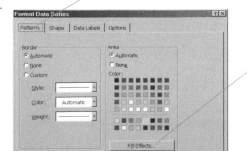

2 Click Fill Effects

6 Click here

3 Click a tab (see the HOT TIPS)

Re step 3 – click Gradient to apply a graduated fill, Texture a textured fill or Pattern a basic pattern.

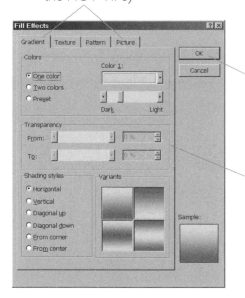

5 Click here

4 Complete the appropriate settings – available options vary according to the tab chosen in step 3

You can also use pictures as fills. Select the Picture tab in step 3. Click the Select Picture button. Now use the Select Picture dialog to locate and double-click the relevant image. Finally, carry out step 5.

Bordering chart components

Changing the line width/border style

In Normal view, go to the slide which hosts the chart you want to amend. Double-click the chart. Now double-click the chart component you want to reformat. Carry out step 1 below. Follow 2–3 to apply a line style; 4–5 to apply a line colour; and/or 6–7 to specify a line thickness.

Finally, perform step 8:

To add a text box to a chart, first double-click it. Now click this button on the Drawing toolbar:

Drag out the text box then insert the relevant text. Press Esc when you've finished.

To format all text in a text box, right-click anywhere on its frame. (To format specific text, select it first inside the frame.) In the menu, click Font. Complete the Font dialog.

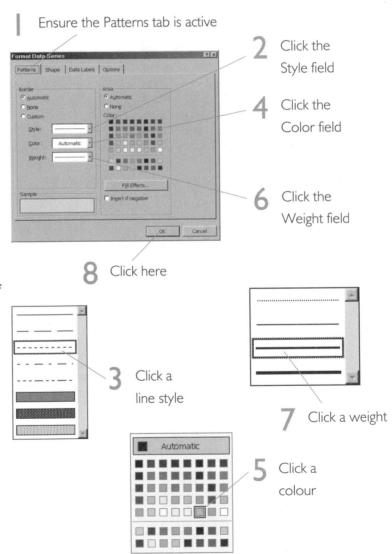

1 Ensure the Patterns tab is active

2 Click the Style field

4 Click the Color field

6 Click the Weight field

8 Click here

3 Click a line style

7 Click a weight

5 Click a colour

Formatting text components

Applying a typeface/type size

In Normal view, go to the slide which hosts the chart you want to amend. Double-click the chart. Now carry out step 1. Follow steps 2–5, as appropriate, then perform step 6:

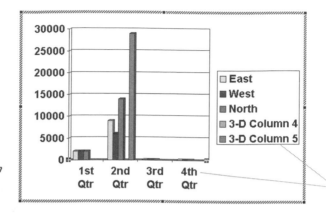

Re step 1 – here, we're selecting a legend. If you double-click an axis, the resultant dialog is slightly different.

To align text in an axis, select the Alignment tab. Select a text orientation and direction and click OK.

You can also embolden and/or italicise text by clicking one of the options in the Font style: field.

Untick Auto scale to stop text and numerical data which have been attached to a chart being automatically resized when you resize the chart.

1 Double-click a text element (e.g. a legend or chart axis)

2 Ensure the Font tab is active

3 Select a typeface

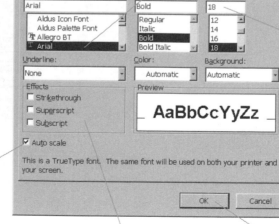

4 Enter a type size

5 Select one or more effects

6 Click OK

Using multimedia

In this chapter, you'll insert clip art/pictures into slides and learn about the formats (bitmap and vector) which PowerPoint recognises. You'll rescale, border, crop, recolour and compress images, and organise clips in your own Clip Organizer collections. You'll allocate keywords to clips, so you can find them easily, download clips from the web and email them to colleagues/friends. Finally, you'll insert sound/film clips and diagrams/org charts into slides and save slides as pictures.

Covers

Chapter Six

Multimedia – an overview

You can add clip art with the use of slide placeholders – see page 124.

PowerPoint 2002 lets you enhance presentations in a variety of ways. You can add:

- clip art

- third-party pictures

- diagrams

- org charts

- sound clips

- video clips

Once you've inserted clip art and pictures, you can also animate them – see chapter 9.

You can also use the Organizer to organise clips, by:

- *moving/copying clips between collections*
- *renaming or deleting collections*
- *searching for specific clips*
- *adding new clips*
- *removing unwanted clips*

You can import sound clips, video clips and clip art via the Clip Organizer. This is a computerised scrapbook which helps you access (and organise) multimedia files. It's a centralised location from which you can interact with, and housekeep, your entire multimedia collection. You don't have to use the Clip Organizer to insert clips into slides, but it does make it easier to locate the clip you want to use.

You can also use the Insert Clip Art Task Pane as a 'window' onto the Organizer. Use this Task Pane as a shortcut, a way to find and utilise clips in the Organizer with even less effort.

You can also add third-party pictures to your slides. These can be:

- output from other programs (e.g. drawings and illustrations)

- commercial clip art

- scanned images/photographs

Inserting clip art

Once inserted into a slide, pictures can be resized and moved in the normal way.

Inserting clip art via the Insert Clip Art Task Pane

In Normal or Notes Page views, go to the slide into which you want the clip art added. Pull down the Insert menu and click Picture, Clip Art. Now carry out the following steps:

Enter one or more keywords

Clips have associated keywords. You can use these to locate clips.

3 Click Search

2 Optional – click here and make the appropriate choices

You can add new clips to collections (or add new keywords to existing clips) in the Clip Organizer. Click here to launch it: then see later in this chapter.

To conduct another search, click the Modify button then repeat steps 1–3.

4 Click an icon to insert the clip

For access to more clips, click Clips Online and follow the on-screen instructions.

Providing the relevant slide has an associated layout which incorporates a clip art placeholder, you can use this to make inserting an image even easier.

Adding clip art via placeholders

In Normal or Notes Page view, go to the slide into which you want the clip art added. Carry out the following:

Re step 1 – some slide layouts have a different placeholder. Do the following:

Click here

Click here

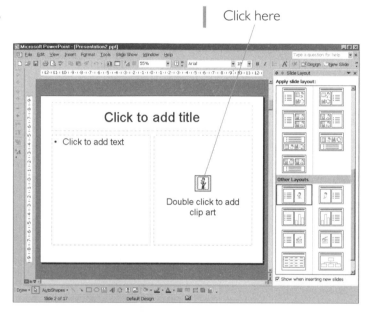

To find more clips, click Import. Use the Add Clips to Organizer dialog to locate and add more clips.

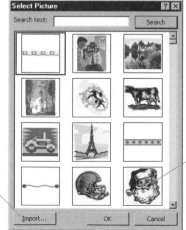

2 Double-click a clip

Working with the Clip Organizer

By default, the Clip Organizer comes with numerous pre-defined collections e.g.

- Business

- Character Collections

- Communication

- Fantasy

- People

Launching the Clip Organizer

If the Clip Organizer isn't already open, pull down the Insert menu and do the following:

You can also start Organizer outside PowerPoint. Choose Start, Programs, Microsoft Office Tools, Microsoft Clip Organizer.

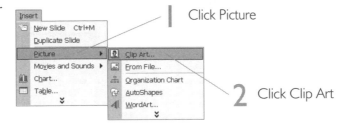

| Click Picture

2 Click Clip Art

You can launch Organizer from within most Office XP modules. Simply follow steps 1–3.

3 Click Clip Organizer

Inserting clips via the Organizer

You can access clips on the web by clicking the following Organizer toolbar button:

Microsoft's Design Gallery Live site launches:

Use this to locate and download extra clips.

To remove a clip from the Organizer (but not your hard disk), right-click it. In the menu, click Delete from Clip Organizer. In the message which launches, click OK.

To add an AutoShape or WordArt object (or any picture created in any other Office module) to the Organizer, select it. Press Ctrl+C. In the Organizer, go to the collection folder you want to add it to and press Shift+Insert – a copy of the object is inserted as a clip.

You can use the Clip Organizer to insert clip art into your slides. This is a useful technique.

1 If the Clip Organizer isn't currently open, follow steps 1–3 on page 125

3 Drag a clip onto your slide

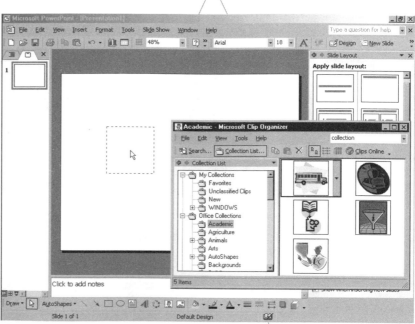

2 Click a collection

4 Resize and/or reposition the picture in the usual way

Creating new collections

To have Organizer search for media files and organize them into collections for you (see My Collections here), choose File, Add Clips to Organizer, Automatically. In the dialog, click OK.

(When you start Organizer for the first time, it offers to carry out this procedure for you.)

To manually add a clip to the Organizer, pull down the File menu and click Add Clips to Organizer, On My Own. Use the Add Clips to Organizer dialog to locate and select the clip you want to add (first ensure the Files of type: field shows the correct format e.g. Pictures). Now click Add To. In the Import to Collection dialog, select a host collection. Click OK.

Finally, back in the Add Clips to Organizer dialog, click Add.

You can only create a new collection from within My Collections.

To create a new collection, do the following:

1 If the Clip Organizer isn't currently open, follow steps 1–3 on page 125

2 Click Collection List, then select My Collections

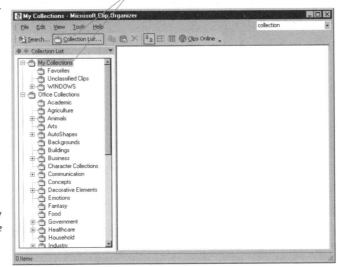

3 Pull down the File menu and click New Collection

5 Name the collection

4 Select a destination folder

6 Click here

Renaming collections

1 If the Clip Organizer isn't currently open, follow steps 1–3 on page 125

When Clip Organizer creates collections automatically, their names are based on the host folders. You can easily rename these...

2 Right-click a folder under My Collections

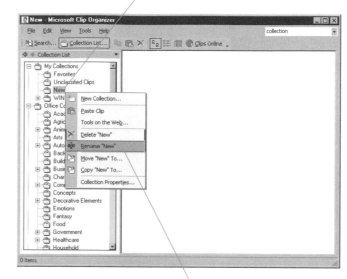

You can't rename the collections supplied with Clip Organizer.

To delete a collection, follow steps 1-2. In step 3, select Delete...
In the message, click Yes.

3 Click Rename...

When you delete a collection (see the above tip), the associated clips are not deleted.

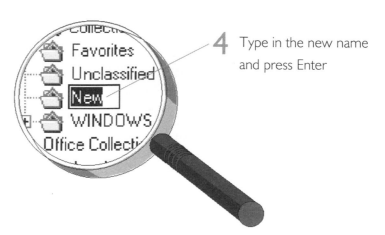

4 Type in the new name and press Enter

To preview a clip, right-click it in the Organizer (or after a search in the Insert Clip Art Task Pane) and select Preview/ Property. Press Esc when you're through.

Using keywords

When clips are added to Clip Organizer (either manually or automatically – see the HOT TIPs on page 127), certain keywords are routinely added to them. These are based on the name or suffix, but you may want to add your own keywords (so you can locate the clips more easily later).

Clips in the Clip Organizer can (and do) have keywords associated with them (this means, for instance, that if you want to find a specific picture you can run a keyword search – see page 130). You can add additional keywords to any clip.

Adding keywords to a clip

Do the following:

I   If the Clip Organizer isn't currently open, follow steps 1–3 on page 125

To find related clips, right-click a clip in the Organizer (or after a search in the Insert Clip Art Task Pane) and select Find Similar Style.

2   Select a collection

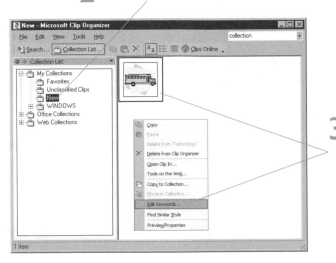

3   Right-click a clip; in the menu, select Edit Keywords

To change an existing keyword, select it in the Keywords for current clip field. Amend the keyword in the Keyword box and click Modify.
To delete a keyword, highlight it in the Keywords for current clip field and click Delete. The keyword is removed immediately.

4   Enter a new keyword and click Add

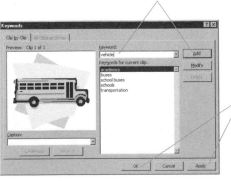

5   Click OK or Apply

You can use a shortcut to email a clip to someone. Choose File, Send to Mail Recipient (as Attachment). Complete the New Message dialog and click Send.

Searching for keywords

You can also run a search from the Insert Clip Art Task Pane. Follow steps 3–4 (and see the tip below).

To search for clips by one or more keywords, do the following:

1 If the Clip Organizer isn't open, follow steps 1–3 on page 125

2 Click Search

3 Enter keyword(s) – see the DON'T FORGET tips on the facing page

If you want to customise the search, do one or both of the following:

• click here; in the list, select a collection to search in (e.g. Office Collections, or specify an individual collection)

• click here; in the list, specify a search format (e.g. Clip Art or Sounds, or specify a precise format)

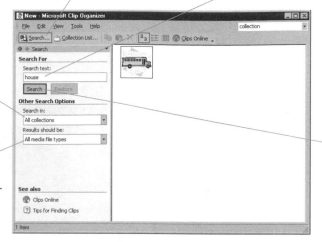

4 Click Search

Moving the mouse pointer over a clip produces a box listing the first few associated keywords:

Earth, environmental awareness...
213 (w) x 263 (h) pixels, 31 KB, WMF

The end result:

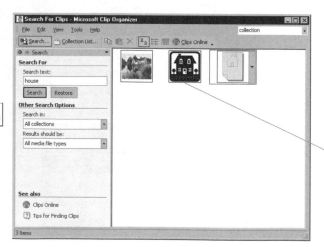

The flagged clips display

If your web connection is live when you run a search, PowerPoint automatically searches content on Microsoft's Design Gallery Live site.

Inserting pictures – an overview

Re step 3 on the facing page – you can also search for filenames.

Additionally, you can use standard wildcards – for example, to find all BMP files, type in:

*.bmp

Alternatively, to locate a clip called 'plane1.tif' (but not 'plane12.tif'), search for:

plane?.tif

(The last method would also find 'plane5.tif' and 'plane8.tif'.)

Re step 3 on the facing page – the table below illustrates the syntax you can use:

To find the unconnected keywords *red* and *bus*	Type in: red bus
To find the phrase *red bus*	Type in: "red bus"
To find *red* or *bus*	Type in: red, bus

See page 132 for details of specific bitmap and vector formats PowerPoint 2002 recognises.

Pictures PowerPoint 2002 can import into slides fall into two overall categories:

- bitmap images

- vector images

The following are brief details of each (note particularly that there is a certain level of crossover between the two formats):

Bitmap images

Bitmaps consist of pixels (dots) arranged in such a way that they form a graphic image. Because of the very nature of bitmaps, the question of 'resolution' – the sharpness of an image expressed in dpi (dots per inch) – is very important. Bitmaps look best if they're displayed at their correct resolution. You should bear this in mind if you're exporting files from other programs for inclusion in PowerPoint 2002 slides.

PowerPoint 2002 imports (i.e. translates into its own format) a wide variety of third-party bitmap formats.

Vector images

PowerPoint 2002 will also import vector graphics files in formats native to other programs. Vector images consist of, and are defined by, algebraic equations. One practical result of this is that they can be rescaled without any loss of definition. Another corollary is that they're less complex than bitmaps: they contain less detail.

Vector files can also include bitmap information. For example, PostScript files often have an illustrative header (used for preview purposes) which is generally a low-resolution bitmap. This header is very often considerably inferior in quality when compared to the underlying picture.

Picture formats

Many bitmap formats have compression as an option. This allows bitmaps – often very large – to be stored on disk in much smaller files.

There are two further much-used graphics formats you should be aware of:

- *Windows Bitmap. A popular format. File suffix: BMP*

- *Windows Metafile. A frequently used vector format. Used for information exchange between just about all Windows programs. File suffix: WMF*

You can save slides or other objects as pictures/ graphics:

- *To save a slide, go to it. Choose File, Save As. In the Save As dialog, select a graphics format. Name the file and save it to the relevant drive/folder*

- *To save one or more objects, select them. Right-click the object(s) and select Save as Picture. In the Save As Picture dialog, select a graphics format. Name the file and save it to the relevant drive/folder*

Graphics formats PowerPoint 2002 will accept include the following (the column on the left shows the relevant file suffix):

CGM Computer Graphics Metafile. A vector format frequently used in the past, especially as a medium for clip-art transmission. Less often used nowadays.

EPS Encapsulated PostScript. Perhaps the most widely used PostScript format. PostScript combines vector *and* bitmap data very successfully. Incorporates a low-resolution bitmap 'header' for preview purposes.

GIF Graphics Interchange Format. A bitmap format developed for the on-line transmission of graphics data over the Internet. Just about any Windows program – and a lot more besides – will read GIF. Disadvantage: it can't handle more than 256 colours. Compression is supported.

JPEG Joint Photographic Experts Group. Used for photograph storage, especially on the web. It supports a very high level of compression, usually without appreciable distortion.

PCD (Kodak) PhotoCD. Used primarily to store photographs on CD.

PCX An old stand-by. Originated with PC Paintbrush, a paint program. A bitmap format used for years to transfer graphics data between Windows applications.

PNG Interlaced Portable Network Graphics. Used occasionally on the web.

TGA Targa. A high-end bitmap format, and also a bridge with so-called low-end computers (e.g. Amiga and Atari). Often used in PC and Mac paint and ray-tracing programs because of its high-resolution colour fidelity.

TIFF Tagged Image File Format. Suffix: TIF. A bitmap format and, if anything, even more widely used than PCX, across a whole range of platforms and applications.

Inserting pictures

To have a picture appear on every slide, insert it into the slide master (a template which applies to the overall slide show).

Pull down the View menu and click Master, Slide Master. Now insert a picture. To return to the active slide, do the following:

Click here

See pages 73–76 for more on masters.

Re steps 1–2 – choose Picture, From Scanner or Camera instead to insert input from a scanner or camera. Now select the relevant device and follow the on-screen instructions.

PowerPoint 2002 provides a preview of what the picture will look like when it's been imported – see the Preview box on the right of the dialog.

If this isn't visible, click the following toolbar icon repeatedly until it is:

In Normal or Notes Page views, go to the slide into which you want the picture added. Pull down the Insert menu and do the following:

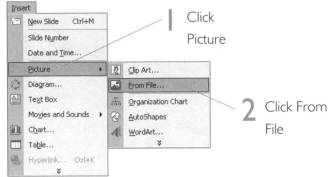

1 Click Picture

2 Click From File

4 Click here. In the drop-down list, click the drive/folder that hosts the picture

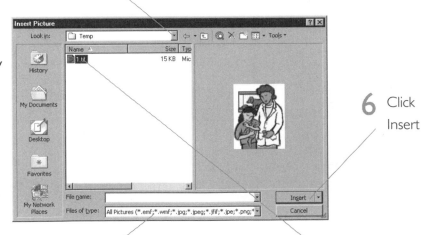

6 Click Insert

3 Make sure All Pictures... is showing. If it isn't, click the arrow and select it from the drop-down list

5 Click a picture file (to import more than one, hold down Ctrl as you click them)

Working with clip art/pictures

If the Picture toolbar isn't currently on-screen, pull down the View menu and click Toolbars, Picture.

You can perform the following actions on clip art/pictures:

- resizing/cropping

- recolouring (but not in respect of imported bitmaps)

- bordering

Resizing clip art/pictures

In Normal or Notes Pages view, select the clip art/picture. Now do the following:

You can't crop animated GIF files – see the facing page.

Drag any handle inwards or outwards

Re step 1 – the following table displays some tips to help you crop more effectively:

Cropping clip art/pictures

In Normal or Notes Pages view, select the image. Refer to the Picture toolbar (it launches automatically) and do the following:

Click here

To crop from two sides at once	Hold down Ctrl as you drag in one centre handle
To crop from all sides at once	As above, but drag in a corner handle

2 Move the mouse pointer over any of the image handles and drag in to crop. Release the mouse button:

To undo a crop (unless you've compressed the image), press Ctrl+Z.

You can also use another method. Double-click the image. In the Format Picture dialog, select the Picture tab then click Reset. Click OK.

Before...

After

If the Picture toolbar isn't currently on-screen, pull down the View menu and click Toolbars, Picture.

Many of the effects applied to AutoShapes (see pages 98-100) can also be applied to pictures. For example, you can shadow them and make them 3D...

You can have PowerPoint compress images within slides (so your presentations use less hard disk space).

Select the image then click this button in the Picture toolbar:

Complete the Compress Pictures dialog – for instance:

- *select whether compression should apply to all images in the presentation*
- *specify whether unused portions of images should be deleted (by default, PowerPoint retains hidden data when you crop pictures – see page 134)*

Finally, click OK.

Recolouring clip art/pictures

In Normal or Notes Pages view, select the clip art/picture. Now refer to the Picture toolbar and do the following:

1 Click here

2 Click the colour you want to change

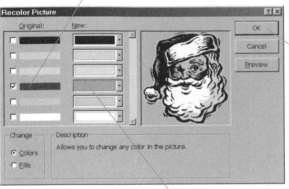

5 Click OK

3 Click the box on the right

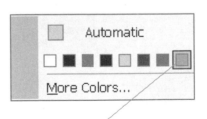

4 Select a new colour

By default, PowerPoint 2002 does not apply a border to inserted clip art/pictures. However, you can apply a wide selection of borders if you want. You can specify:

- the border style

- the border thickness

- the border colour

- whether the border is dashed

Applying a border

First, select the image you want to border. Then pull down the Format menu and click Picture. Now carry out step 1 below. Perform 2–3, as appropriate. Finally, carry out step 4:

1 Ensure the Colors and Lines tab is active

To specify a border width, click in the Weight field and type in a new width in points (1 inch is roughly equivalent to 72 points).

Re step 3 – if you want to apply a dotted (as opposed to a straight) border, click in the Dashed field instead and select one in the list.

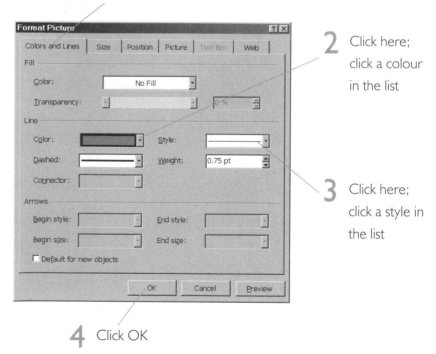

2 Click here; click a colour in the list

3 Click here; click a style in the list

4 Click OK

You can also use the Picture toolbar to adjust image brightness and/or contrast.

Amending brightness/contrast

In Normal or Notes Pages view, select the clip art/picture. Now refer to the Picture toolbar and do the following:

1 | Click here

2 Ensure the Picture tab is active

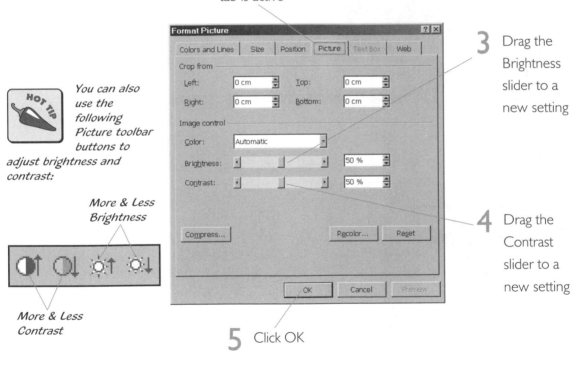

3 Drag the Brightness slider to a new setting

4 Drag the Contrast slider to a new setting

5 Click OK

You can also use the following Picture toolbar buttons to adjust brightness and contrast:

More & Less Brightness

More & Less Contrast

Inserting diagrams

Re step 2 – clicking the flagged item produces an org chart. For details of additional diagram types see the table below:

Cycle	For continuous processes
Target	Best at showing progressive steps
Radial	Shows relationships between related events and a central core
Venn	Best at showing overlapping areas
Pyramid	Best at showing 'bottom-up' relationships

You can insert diagrams (e.g. pyramids and org charts) into slides.

In Normal or Notes Page view, pull down the Insert menu and click Diagram

2 Click a diagram

3 Click here

Clicking a text placeholder or the diagram itself launches the Diagram toolbar. Use this to make any further changes e.g.:

Click Change to to transform the diagram into another

Click Layout to make layout changes

You can also create flowcharts (by creating AutoShapes using the Flowchart and Connectors categories) – see pages 97–101.

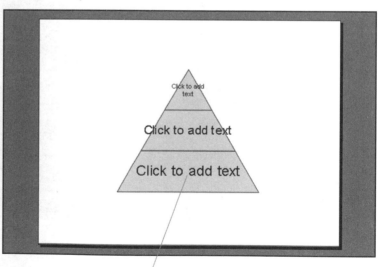

An inserted pyramid – edit it as required e.g. click a text placeholder and type in text

Inserting sound clips

Sound clips can enhance slide impact tremendously.

Adding sound clips to slides

In Normal view, go to the slide you want to insert the sound clip into. Now pull down the Insert menu and click Movies and Sounds, Sound from Clip Organizer. Carry out the following:

To insert sound or movie clips into the Organizer, follow the procedures in the HOT TIPs on page 127.

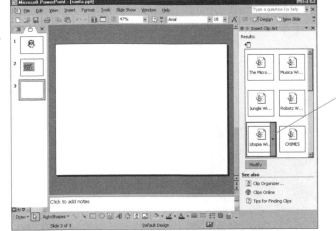

Click here; in the menu, select Insert

You must have a sound card installed in your PC to play sound clips.

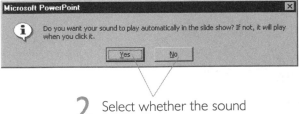

You can also insert sound files into a slide. Pull down the Insert menu and click Movies and Sounds, Sound from File. In the Insert Sound dialog, locate and click a sound file. Click OK then complete step 2.

2 Select whether the sound clip should auto-play

Playing sound clips

Double-click here to manually play a sound clip

Inserting video clips

Note that you can also insert video clips via the Clip Organizer.

Pull down the Insert menu and click Movies and Sounds, Movie from Clip Organizer. In the Insert Clip Art Task Pane, find the movie clip you want to insert, then right-click it. In the menu, click Insert. In the message, perform step 4 OR 5.

Re step 2 – you can also carry out one of the following procedures:

- *Windows NT 4 and 98 users – use Network Neighborhood to import from a local network folder and Web Folders to import from a web/FTP folder*

- *Windows 2000 and Me users – use My Network Places to import from a local network folder or from a web/FTP folder*

Re step 3 – you may have to double-click one or more folders first, to locate the movie file.

To manually play a video clip within a slide, simply double-click it.

Video clips introduce a welcome note of animation into slides.

Adding video clips to slides

In Normal view, go to the slide into which you want to insert the video clip. Now pull down the Insert menu and click Movies and Sounds, Movie from File. Carry out the following steps:

2 Click here. In the drop-down list, click the drive that hosts the movie

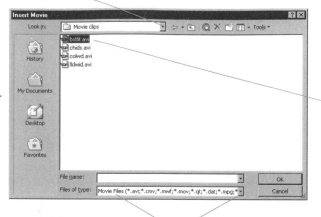

3 Double-click a movie file

Make sure Movie Files... is showing. If it isn't, click the arrow and select it from the drop-down list

4 Click Yes to have the clip play automatically when you run your slide show

5 Click No if you want to play the clip manually

Using speech recognition

Dictating text into PowerPoint 2002 provides a valuable alternative way to input it – you can also use speech recognition to enter commands etc.

First, you'll carry out a custom install, to install speech recognition for use with PowerPoint. Then you'll 'train' the software, so it's set up for your voice and dictating conditions. You'll go on to dictate content into PowerPoint 2002 and have it turned into on-screen text. When errors occur, you'll correct them with the mouse and keyboard (in the usual way) or dictate the replacement.

Finally, you'll launch menus, toolbar buttons, dialogs and the Task Pane with dedicated voice commands.

Covers

Chapter Seven

Preparing to use speech recognition

To use speech recognition, you need the following:

- *a high-quality headset, preferably with USB (Universal Serial Bus) support and gain adjustment*

- *a minimum chip speed of 400 MHz (slower chips make dictation extremely laborious)*

- *a minimum of 128 Mb of RAM*

- *Windows 98 (or NT 4.0) or later*

- *Internet Explorer 5.0 (or later)*

For more information on requirements, visit (no spaces or line breaks):

http://office.microsoft.com/ assistance/2002/articles/ oSpeechRequirements_aw.htm

The Microphone Wizard only launches the first time you follow step 1 (after this, step 1 activates speech recognition).

Your use of speech recognition will benefit from repeated training. Click the Tools button on the Language Bar and select Training. Complete the wizard which launches.

Installing/running speech recognition

If you haven't already done so, you must first run a custom install. In Control Panel, double-click Add/Remove Programs. Select Microsoft Office XP... Click Add/Remove, then Add or Remove Features, Next. Double-click Office Shared Features, then Alternative User Input. Select Speech then the type of installation you need. Click Update.

Preparing speech recognition

Before you can dictate into PowerPoint 2002, you have to adjust your microphone and carry out a brief 'training' procedure to acclimatise PowerPoint to the sound of your voice:

| Choose Tools, Speech

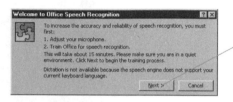

2 Click Next to begin the training process

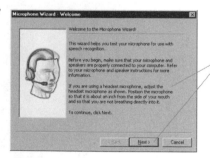

3 Adjust your microphone in line with the instructions then click Next

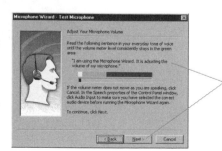

4 Read out the sentence shown then click Next. Complete the rest of the wizard – it should take about 15 minutes

Dictating text

If you run speech recognition in less than optimal conditions, the results may well be poor.

1 Follow step one on page 142

2 If the microphone isn't already turned on, click here

3 The Language bar expands – click Dictation

To get the best out of speech recognition, you need to carry out the following:

- *keep your environment as quiet as possible*
- *keep the microphone in the same position relative to your mouth*
- *run the training wizard as often as possible*
- *pronounce words clearly but don't pause between them or between individual letters – only pause at the end of your train of thought*
- *turn off the microphone when not in use (by repeating step 1)*

4 Begin dictating. Initially, PowerPoint inserts a blue bar on the screen – the text appears as soon as it's recognised:

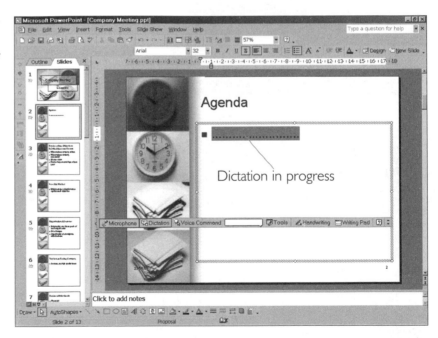

For the best results, use speech recognition in conjunction with mouse and keyboard use.

5 To close speech recognition when you've finished, repeat step 1

Entering voice commands

You can switch to Voice Command by saying 'Voice Command', or dictation by saying 'Dictation'.

Commands you speak appear in the following Language bar field:

For more details of voice commands, see the HELP topic 'Getting started with speech recognition'.

1   Follow step 1 on page 142

2   Click Voice Command

3   Issue the appropriate command using the following as guides:

- to launch the File menu say 'file' or 'file menu' (to select a menu entry say the name)
- to open the Font dialog say 'font' (to select a typeface, say the name)
- to close a dialog say 'OK'
- to select a toolbar button, say the name
- to launch the New File Task Pane, say 'file' then 'new'

Correcting errors

If the Language Bar isn't visible or minimised on the Taskbar, go to Control Panel. Double-click Text Services. In the dialog, click Language Bar. Select Show the Language bar on the desktop. Click OK twice.

1   Replace wrong text with corrections in the usual way

2   Or select the error with your mouse . In Dictation mode, say 'spelling mode'. Pause, then spell out the substitution e.g. o-n-c-e

3   Or select the error with your mouse (it's best to also select one or two correct words on either side of the error). In Dictation mode, say the words you selected

Re step 3 – it's best to correct phrases rather than individual words.

Finalising slide shows

In this chapter, you'll fine-tune your presentation before you get ready to run it. You'll add (and print) summary slides, comments, speaker notes and handouts. You'll also export handouts and outlines to Microsoft Word 2002, because of its greater formatting capabilities. You'll apply the correct page setup parameters to your slide show; specify the correct printer setup; and then launch Print Preview so you can proof your presentation on-screen.

Finally, you'll print out your slide show and all its components.

Covers

Chapter Eight

Fine-tuning your slide show

When you've finished developing your presentation (using the techniques discussed in earlier chapters), you should consider adding some last minute enhancements before you prepare it to be run. You can:

Summary slides list the main sections in your presentation for ease of access.

For how to create summary slides, see the HOT TIP on page 56. For how to insert hyperlinks (to make the summary slide even more useful), see Chapter 9.

- create summary slides (see the DON'T FORGET tip on the left)

- insert internal comments

- add speaker notes

- create handouts

Internal comments aid the review/correction process by allowing presentations to be annotated by multiple users.

Speaker notes are a 'script' which you can create in Notes Page view (or in Notes view within Normal view) to help you give the presentation. Many PowerPoint 2002 users find these scripts very useful, even indispensable.

Handouts, on the other hand, are printed material which you supply to the slide show audience. Handouts consist of the following:

- an outline which the audience can follow as you speak

- copies of the individual slides (printed one or more to the page)

Additional preparations include:

- specifying page setup parameters

- specifying printer setup parameters

- printing out a proof copy of the presentation

- exporting slides or outlines to Word 2002

Comments – an overview

If your presentation requires to be reviewed, you can insert the necessary comments into the relevant slides. When you've done this, other users can review your annotations, as appropriate. Alternatively, you can simply insert comments for your own information. For example, if you're not sure about the design of a particular slide but want to move on to the next, you could insert a comment (for your own attention) as a reminder that you need to go back to the original slide and review it later...

PowerPoint 2002 comments are self-formatting, self-wrapping text boxes with associated markers:

Comment marker

| SC3 | **S. Copestake** | 21/08/01 |

Note:

Should we use 'Market Evaluation' rather than 'Market Summary' here?

Sample comment

If anyone else edits your comment, their initials are inserted and PowerPoint then regards them as the author of the comment.

When you create a comment, PowerPoint 2002 automatically inserts your name – in bold – at the start. When you type in the comment text, the box wraps around the text.

Fine-tuning comments

When you've inserted comments, you can:

- resize them

- edit them

- view/hide them

- delete them if they've been actioned and are no longer required

Inserting a comment

In Normal view, go to the slide into which you want to insert the comment. Pull down the Insert menu and do the following:

 When you carry out step 1, all comments previously inserted into the current slide become visible.

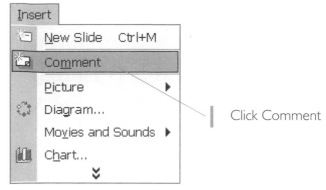

Click Comment

 To move a comment to another location, select its marker:

Drag the marker elsewhere in the slide.

PowerPoint 2002 inserts a new comment, complete with your name as the author. Do the following:

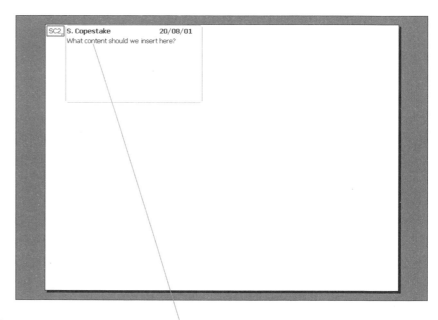

 To resize a (completed) comment box, select it. Then use standard Windows resizing techniques.

 To print out pages containing comments, select Include comment pages in the Print dialog (see page 160).

2 Type in your comment, then click outside the comment box

Working with comments

If the Reviewing toolbar isn't currently on-screen, pull down the View menu and click Toolbars, Reviewing.

Viewing/hiding comment markers

To make comment markers visible or invisible (depending on the current setting), refer to the Reviewing toolbar and do the following:

Click here

To view previous or subsequent comments, click the following in the Reviewing toolbar:

Previous comment

Next comment

Note, however, that when you carry out step 1, the effects are global: all slides within the current slide show are affected.

Viewing specific comments

Click here to activate the marker (to edit the contents, see the HOT TIP)

To edit a comment, double-click its marker. Click in the comment then make the necessary changes. When you've finished, click back in the slide itself.

Deleting comments

Ensure comment markers are currently visible (see above). Then carry out the following steps:

1   Select the marker and press Delete

 S. Copestake   **20/08/01**
What content should we insert here?
Should we change 'Market Evaluation' to 'Market Summary'?

To delete all comments on the active slide, carry out the following on the Reviewing toolbar:

Click here; select Delete All Markers on the Current Slide

2   PowerPoint 2002 deletes the comment straightaway, without launching a warning message first. However, you can undo the deletion by pressing Ctrl+Z

Working with speaker notes

Every PowerPoint 2002 slide has a corresponding Notes page which displays:

- a reduced-size version of the slide

- a notes section complete with a notes placeholder

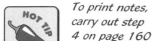

If you have trouble working with note placeholders, try increasing the Zoom size.

Pull down the View menu and click Zoom. Click a higher zoom %. Click OK.

You can use the placeholder to enter notes which you'll refer to (either on-screen or from a printed copy) as you give your presentation.

You can create notes in the following ways:

- from within Notes Page view

- from within Normal view

Adding speaker notes within Notes Page view

To print notes, carry out step 4 on page 160 (but select Notes Pages in the drop-down list).

If you're not already using Notes Page view, pull down the View menu and click Notes Page. Go to the slide into which you want to enter notes. Now do the following:

To print an outline, first ensure it shows the correct levels (by promoting/demoting etc. as necessary – see pages 53-56). Now carry out step 4 on page 160 (but select Outline View in the drop-down list).

(Note that outlines may look different when printed – this is because all formatting attributes automatically print.)

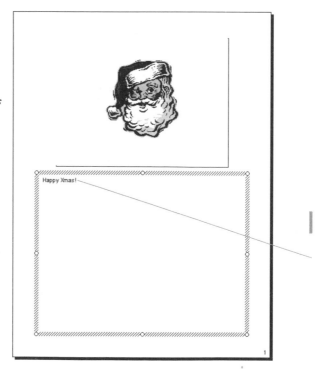

Click in the placeholder. Type in your notes, then click outside the placeholder

If you're already in Normal view, simply carry out steps 2–3.

Adding speaker notes within Normal view

If you're not already using Normal view, pull down the View menu and do the following.

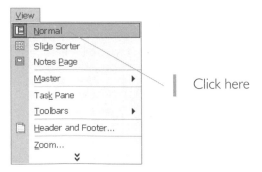

Click here

If you want to add text or pictures to all notes pages, add them to the Notes master.

Pull down the View menu and click Master, Notes Master. Click in the note placeholder; add the relevant text and/or picture in the normal way. Finally, carry out the following:

2 Go to the slide into which you want to enter notes

Click here

To view note formatting accurately, click this button in the Standard toolbar (or fly-out):

Notes view

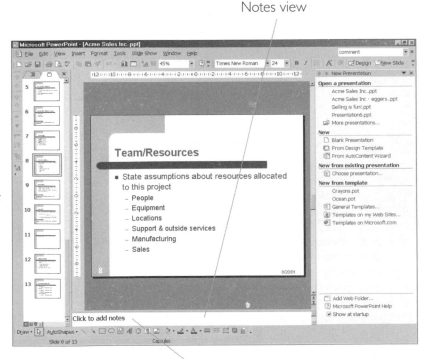

3 Type in the note text

Handouts

You create handouts with the help of the Handouts master.

Creating a handout

Pull down the View menu and do the following:

You can specify the number of slides per page. Refer to the Handout Master toolbar and click:

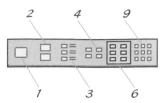

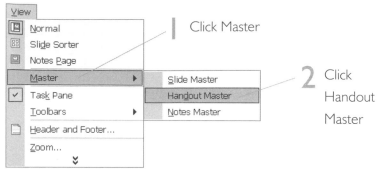

1 Click Master

2 Click Handout Master

PowerPoint 2002 now launches the Handout master (with specific items – e.g. page numbers and footer text – already included):

To print handouts, carry out step 4 on page 160 (but select Handouts in the drop-down list).

Handout Master toolbar

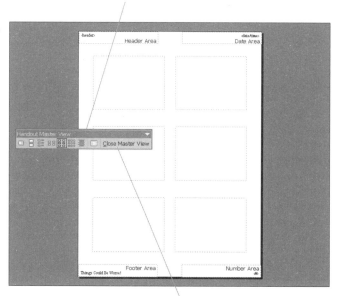

Before you carry out step 3, consider doing the following:

- *click in the Header Area and replace <header> with the relevant header text*
- *click in the Date area and replacing <date/time> with a specific date/time*

Alternatively, amend the footer text as appropriate.

3 Click Close Master View to close the Handout master

Exporting handouts to Word 2002

If the procedures listed on page 152 aren't adequate (for instance, if the presentation you're developing also involves a manual), you can create your handout in Word. When you do this, PowerPoint 2002 transfers all notes/slides automatically while letting you choose the handout format. You can then use the greater formatting capabilities innate in Word 2002 to produce the handout you need.

Exporting to Word 2002

Pull down the File menu and carry out the following steps:

You can also send an outline to Word 2002. First ensure it shows the correct levels (by promoting/ demoting etc. as necessary – see pages 53–56). Now follow steps 1–2. In step 3, select Outline only. Perform steps 4–5.

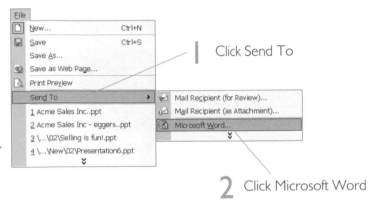

Click Send To

2 Click Microsoft Word

If you want your slide show updated to take account of any changes you make in Word 2002 (see page 154), click Paste link:

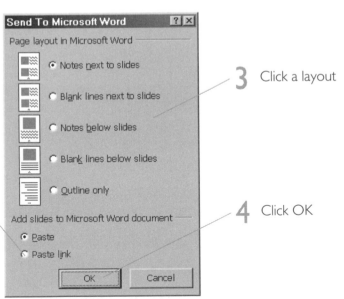

3 Click a layout

4 Click OK

PowerPoint 2002 now starts Word (if it isn't already running) and:

- creates a new document

- inserts your presentation (with the requested layout) into the new document

Do the following:

The inserted presentation

If you need help with using Word, consider buying one of these companion volumes:

- *Word 2000 in easy steps*
- *Word 2002 in easy steps*

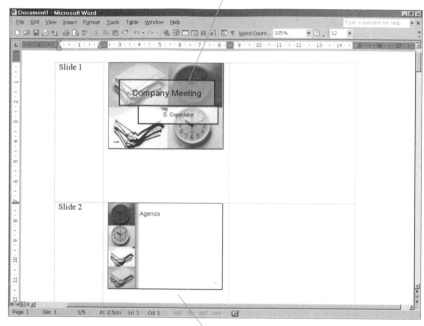

5 Edit the presentation in the normal way

If you clicked Paste link on page 153 (see the HOT TIP on the same page), any editing changes you make in Word are automatically reflected in your original presentation.

Page setup issues

Before you print a slide show, it's a good idea to specify:

- whether you want to print slides in Landscape (the default) or Portrait format

- the dimensions of the printed page

There are two aspects to every page size: a vertical measurement and a horizontal measurement. These can be varied according to orientation. There are two possible orientations:

If you change a slide show's orientation, you'll probably have to adjust items on the slides (e.g. text placeholders) to accommodate the new orientation.

Portrait   Landscape

Re step 1 – you can choose from a variety of paper sizes (e.g. A3 and B5) as well as transparencies.

Specifying page setup options

Pull down the File menu and click Page Setup. Now do the following:

Click here; select a slide size in the list

You can specify the start point from which slides are numbered.

Type in the start number here:

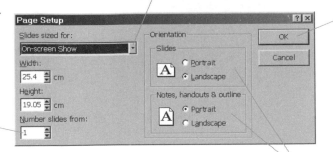

3 Click here

2 Specify an orientation

Re step 2 – all the slides within a given presentation must have the same orientation.

Printer setup

Before you can begin printing out your slide shows, you need to ensure that:

- the correct printer is selected (if you have more than one installed)

- the correct printer settings are in force

PowerPoint 2002 calls these collectively the 'printer setup'.

Irrespective of the printer selected, the settings vary in accordance with the job in hand. For example, most printer drivers (the software which 'drives' the printer) allow you to specify whether or not you want pictures printed. Additionally, they often allow you to specify the resolution or print quality of the output...

Selecting the printer and/or settings

At any time before you're ready to print a presentation, pull down the File menu and click Print. Now do the following:

Click here; select the printer you want from the list

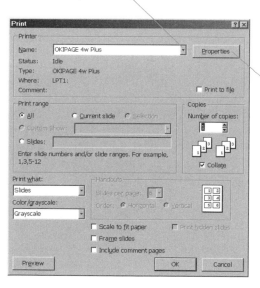

2 Click Properties to adjust printer settings (see your printer's manual for how to do this)

3 Complete the remainder of the Print dialog, prior to printing your slide show (see pages 159–160)

Launching Print Preview

Print Preview displays slides in greyscale (rather than colour).

PowerPoint 2002 provides a special view mode called Print Preview. This displays the active slide as it will look when printed. Use Print Preview as a final check just before you begin printing.

You can perform the following actions from within Print Preview:

- moving from slide to slide

- zooming in or out with the mouse pointer

- zooming to a preset view percentage

- specifying which component prints (you can also do this from the Print dialog – see page 160)

Launching Print Preview

Pull down the File menu and click Print Preview. This is the result:

To leave Print Preview mode and return to your slide show), simply

press Esc.

You can also enter or leave Print Preview by pressing Ctrl+F2.

Special Print Preview toolbar

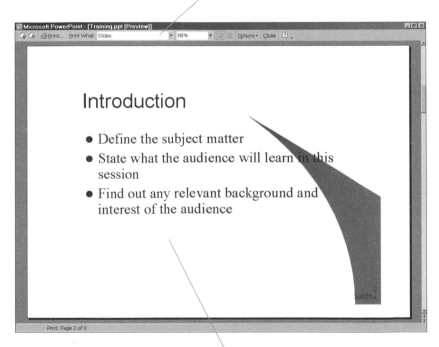

A preview of a presentation

Working with Print Preview

Nearly all of the operations you can perform in Print Preview mode can be accessed via the toolbar.

Using the Print Preview toolbar

Do any of the following, as appropriate:

To print a frame around slides, click the Options button. In the menu, select Frame Slides.

1 Click here to jump to the next slide

3 Click here – in the list, select a Zoom size

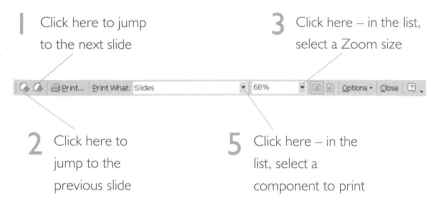

2 Click here to jump to the previous slide

5 Click here – in the list, select a component to print

Using the Zoom cursor

You can also zoom in or out (in a relatively limited way) by using the Zoom cursor.

1 Place the cursor at the appropriate location and left-click once to zoom in or out

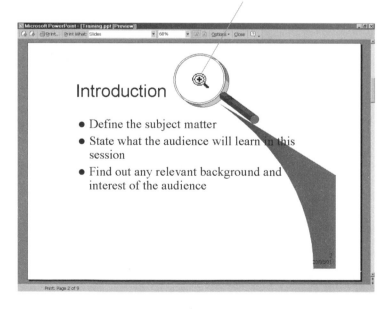

Printing – an overview

You can print any presentation component. These include:

- slides

- notes

- outlines

- handouts

- comments

You can also:

- specify the number of copies

- specify slide ranges (e.g. slides 1–6 inclusive and 11)

- have printed copies collated

- print out slides in greyscale, or black-and-white ('mono')

- proportionately scale printed output up or down to match your paper size

Alternatively, you can simply opt to print your presentation with the current options/settings (PowerPoint 2002 provides a 'fast-track' approach to this).

Collation

Collation is the process whereby PowerPoint 2002 prints one full copy of a presentation at a time. For instance, if you're printing three copies of an 8-slide presentation, PowerPoint 2002 prints slides 1–8 of the first slide show, followed by slides 1–8 of the second and slides 1–8 of the third.

Collation is only possible if you're printing multiple copies of a slide show.

Presentations are intended to be printed in colour, but handouts and notes are generally printed in greyscale or mono.

Mono printing has certain restrictions. For example, bitmapped pictures, clip art and charts always print in greyscale, even if mono is selected.

By default, PowerPoint prints in the background, so you can go on working. However, background printing takes up additional system resources. If you need to disable this, choose Tools, Options. Select the Print tab. Untick Background printing and click OK.

Printing your slide show

First, carry out steps 1–2 on page 156.

Printing a presentation

Pull down the File menu and click Print. Now carry out any of steps 1–4 below, as appropriate. Finally, follow step 5.

Ensure Collate is selected if you want output collated.

Click Current slide to print only the active slide

Click Scale to fit paper to have output scaled evenly to fit your paper size.

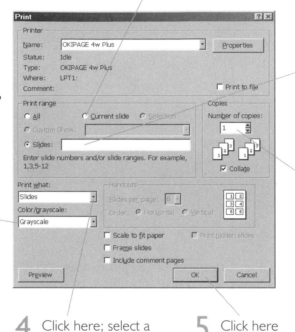

3 Type in a slide range (if appropriate)

2 Type in the no. of copies required

Ensure Grayscale is selected in the Color/grayscale field if you want to print out in greyscale. Click Pure Black and White to print out in mono.

Re step 3 – separate non-adjacent slides with commas (but no comma on the last one) – e.g. to print slides 5, 12 and 16 type in:

5,12,16

Enter contiguous slides with dashes – e.g. to print slides 12 to 23 inclusive, type:

12-23

4 Click here; select a slide show component in the list

5 Click here

Fast-track printing

To print using all the current settings, without launching the Print dialog, simply click the Print button on the Standard toolbar:

Preparing slide shows

In this chapter, you'll get your presentation ready to be run. This involves applying transitions (the process of determining how adjacent slides supersede each other); animations (special effects applied to individual slide objects); and hyperlinks, special buttons or other objects which jump to specific slides or locations (or launch other programs) when you click them. You'll also customise animations in various ways (including changing the animation sequence), stipulate the length of time each slide is on-screen (and turn this off) and rehearse your presentation.

Finally, you'll create custom slide shows for specific audiences and ensure your presentation is set up correctly (including using dual-monitor support, if applicable).

Covers

Preparation – an overview

See Chapter 10 for how to perform – 'run' – slide shows.

PowerPoint 2002 provides a wide assortment of techniques you can use to ensure that your presentation has the maximum impact. These are all ways of preparing your slide show for its eventual performance.

You can:

- specify transitions (interactions between individual slides)

- apply animations (used to control how each slide element is introduced to the audience)

- insert hyperlinks (buttons/objects which – when clicked – jump to additional slides or other targets)

- customise slide timings (the intervals between individual slides)

- customise the presentations setup

Presentation setup

Presentation setup lets you specify:

- which slides do or do not display (via custom slide shows). Use this to prepare presentations which are tailored for specific audiences (some slides may not be suitable for a given recipient) and add hyperlinks where appropriate

- the type of slide show delivery. You can determine whether presentations run:

    — normally (i.e. orchestrated by the presenter)

    — in a special window

    — at a conference kiosk

- whether the presentation runs in 'loop' mode

- whether slides are advanced manually, or using the preset timings

- an alternative screen resolution

- (if you have dual-monitor support) which monitor a presentation runs on

Transitions

Transitions add visual interest to presentations by customising the crossover between individual slides. PowerPoint 2002 provides numerous separate transition effects. These include:

Random Transition	PowerPoint 2002 selects and applies the transition
Blinds Horizontal or Vertical	The next slide displays like a blind
Checkerboard Across or Down	The next slide displays with a chequered pattern
Box In or Out	The next slide displays as an increasing or decreasing box

When you apply a transition to a specific slide, the effect takes place between the previous and selected slides.

You can specify transitions' effects:

- on all slides within a presentation

- on individual slides

Applying transitions to the whole of a slide show

In any view, pull down the Slide Show menu and do the following:

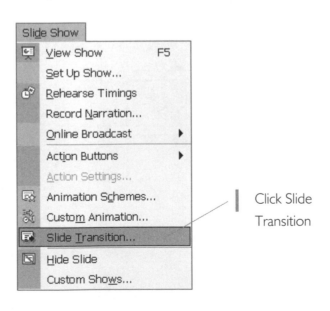

Click Slide Transition

Now carry out the following steps:

In Normal view, you can restrict a transition to the active slide only. Omit step 5. Instead, select a transition here:

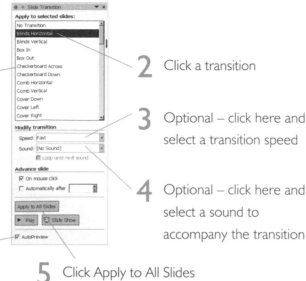

2 Click a transition

3 Optional – click here and select a transition speed

4 Optional – click here and select a sound to accompany the transition

When AutoPreview is ticked, clicking a transition in the Apply to selected slides section previews the effect in the slide itself.

5 Click Apply to All Slides

Applying transitions to multiple slides

In Slide Sorter view, do the following:

If you're not currently in Slide Sorter view, pull down the View menu and click Slide Sorter.

Re step 1 – to select more than one slide, hold down Ctrl as you click the slide icons.

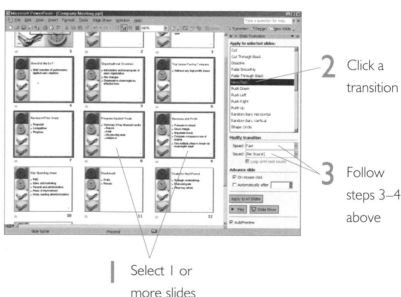

2 Click a transition

3 Follow steps 3–4 above

Select 1 or more slides

Animations

You can use animations to:

• introduce objects onto a slide one at a time (by default, they all appear on-screen at once)

• apply special effects to objects

Having objects appear in a staggered way maximises slide impact; the eye is drawn to areas of specific interest in a way which makes them more prominent.

Imposing special effects on objects is particularly useful:

• to have individual items in a bulleted list appear one at a time

• to have pictures, clip art or charts become prominent slowly

You can apply preset animations or create your own.

Applying a preset animation

In Normal view, pull down the Slide Show menu and click Animation Schemes

You can also apply animations to multiple slides. In Slide Sorter view, select one or more slides. Then choose Slide Show, Animation Schemes and follow step 2.

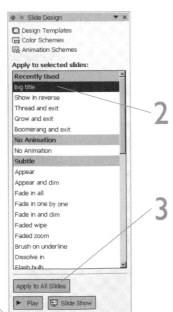

2 Click an animation to apply it to the active slide

When AutoPreview is ticked, clicking an animation in the Apply to selected slides section previews the effect in the slide itself.

3 Alternatively, to apply the animation to every slide, follow step 2 then click Apply to All Slides

Customising animations

In Normal view, right-click the object you want to animate. Pull down the Slide Show menu and click Custom Animation

After you've allocated an effect, configure these fields:

Perform steps 2–4 as often as necessary.

Re steps 3–4 – optionally, select Motion Paths and select a path.

2 Click Add Effect

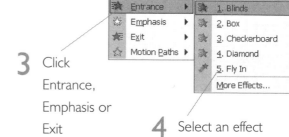

3 Click Entrance, Emphasis or Exit

4 Select an effect

The tags correlate with the animations listed on the right.

Animations display as non-printing tags against the relevant object

Animations are listed here, in the order created

To remove an animation, right-click it in the Task Pane and select Remove in the menu.

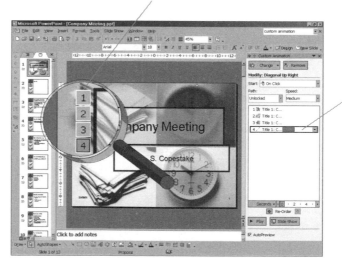

Previewing animations

Previewing also plays any associated sound tracks.

To customise an animation even further, right-click it here:

In the menu, select Effect Options. Select the Effect tab and complete the dialog. Click OK.

1 In Normal view, choose Slide Show, Slide Animation

2 Click Play

To amend an animation, select it in the Task Pane. Click Change.

Follow steps 3–4 on the facing page.

3 PowerPoint runs through all animations in the current slide

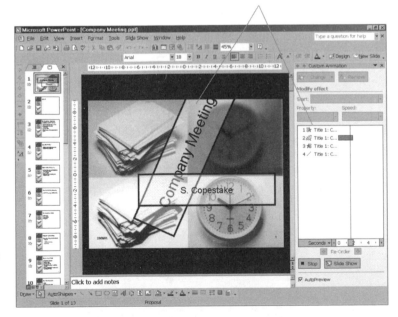

To change the sequence of animations, select one in the Task Pane.

Drag it to a new location in the list.

To change an animation's timing, right-click it in the Task Pane.

Select Timing and complete the Timing dialog.

Inserting hyperlinks

You can insert hyperlinks into slides. In PowerPoint 2002, hyperlinks are 'action buttons' which you can click (while a presentation is being run) to jump to a prearranged destination immediately. This can be:

Text, charts, images and WordArt objects can also be hyperlinks, but action buttons are convenient, ready-made solutions (they're especially suitable for continually running slide shows).

To make any other object a hyperlink, select it. Choose Slide Show, Action Settings. Now follow steps 5–7.

- preset slide targets (for instance, the first, last, next or previous slide)

- a specific slide (where you select a slide from a special dialog)

- a URL (Uniform Resource Locator – these are unique addresses for web sites)

- another PowerPoint presentation

- another file

Inserting an action button

In Normal or Notes Page view, pull down the Slide Show menu. Do the following:

Action buttons are actually AutoShapes. See pages 97–101 for how to work with AutoShapes.

In particular, carry out the procedures in the HOT TIP on page 97 to add identifying text which describes the destination (e.g. 'Slide 13').

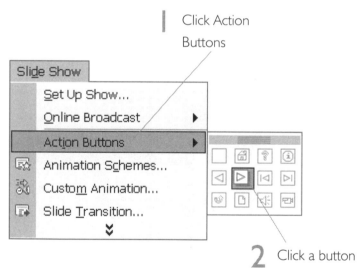

Click Action Buttons

2 Click a button

You can also have action buttons (or other objects) launch external programs in the course of a presentation.

Select the button/object. Pull down the Slide Show menu and click Action Settings. In step 5, select Run program and use the Browse button to locate and double-click the relevant program file. Follow step 7.

3 Place the mouse pointer where you want the button inserted

4 Drag to define the button

...cont'd

Now position the mouse pointer at the location on the slide where you want the button inserted. Hold down the left mouse button and drag to define the button. Release the mouse button and carry out the following steps:

5 Click Hyperlink to:

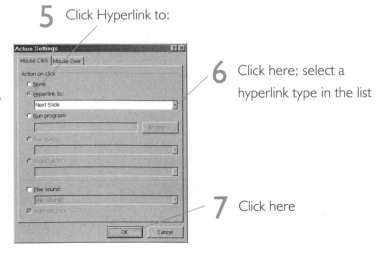

6 Click here; select a hyperlink type in the list

7 Click here

8 The inserted hyperlink

Specifying slide timing

The rehearsal method (a kind of dummy-run) is especially suitable for ensuring that the slide timings you insert are workable.

You can specify how long each slide is on-screen, and by implication the duration of the entire presentation. There are two ways to do this:

- from within Slide Sorter view (either singly, or for every slide)

- by 'rehearsing' the presentation

Applying timings in Slide Sorter view

1 Select one or more slides

2 Pull down the Slide Show menu and click Slide Transition

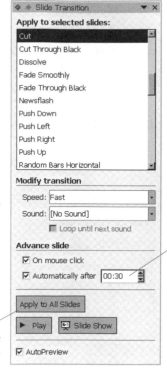

You can follow the procedures here to amend existing timings (or to reset them to zero, if appropriate).

3 Type in a time (in seconds) and press Enter

Click Apply to All Slides to have the timing applied to every slide in the show.

Rehearsing slides uses a special PowerPoint 2002 feature: the Slide Meter.

Applying timings with the Slide Meter

In any view, pull down the Slide Show menu and do the following:

When you've set timings, you can turn them off at will (this doesn't delete them). Follow step 1 on page 174. In the dialog, select Manually in the Advance slides section.

(To reinstate timings, select Using timings, if present.)

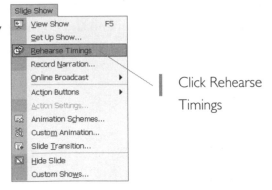

I Click Rehearse Timings

PowerPoint launches its rehearsal window, with the first slide (and the Slide Meter) displayed. Do the following:

Re step 2 – you can also enter times manually:

2 This timer counts the interval until the next slide; when the timing is right, follow step 3

The Slide Meter

If you have one or more custom animations on a slide, step 3 steps through each before moving on to the next slide.

3 Click here

4 PowerPoint moves to the next slide. Repeat steps 2 and 3 until all the slides have had intervals allocated

5 Click Yes

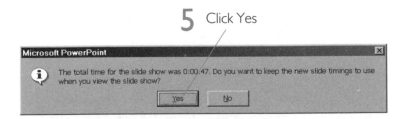

Creating custom slide shows

PowerPoint 2002 lets you create custom slide shows. Custom shows allow you to adopt a mix-and-match approach by selecting specific slides from the active presentation. This allows you to tailor a base slide show for specific audiences and/or occasions.

Creating a custom show

Open the relevant slide show. Select one or more slides, then pull down the Slide Sorter menu and do the following:

For how to run a custom show, see chapter 10.

Click Custom Shows

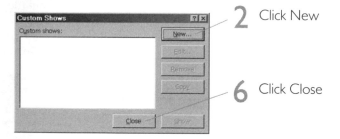

2 Click New

6 Click Close

3 Name the custom show

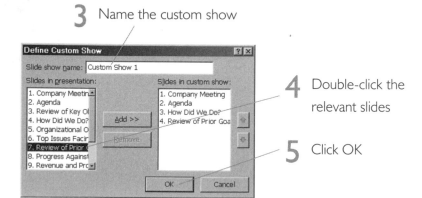

4 Double-click the relevant slides

5 Click OK

Once you've set up a custom slide show, you can:

- add/remove slides

- move slides up or down

Editing a custom show

It's a good idea to combine hyperlinks with custom slide shows.

For example, in one base presentation relating to the whole of a company you could insert a slide with hyperlinks to dedicated slides (each forming a custom show) relating to internal departments...

1 Pull down the Slide Show menu and click Custom Shows

2 Carry out steps 4–5 below. To remove a slide, perform steps 6–7. To change the slide order, follow step 6, and then 8 OR 9. Finally, carry out steps 10–11

4 Click a custom show

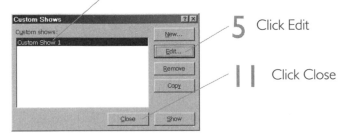

5 Click Edit

11 Click Close

6 Click a slide

To add a new slide to the custom show, double-click it here:

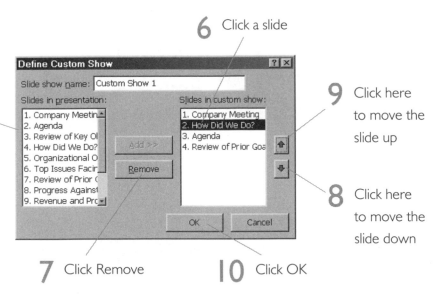

9 Click here to move the slide up

8 Click here to move the slide down

7 Click Remove

10 Click OK

Final preparations

If your PC is set up for dual-monitor support (this means the correct hardware and Windows 98 or later), you can choose the monitor you'll use to display the slide show. Select it in the Multiple monitors section of the Set Up Show dialog.

(Dual-monitor support also gives you access to new Presenter tools – choose Show Presenter View in the dialog.)

The definitive stage in slide show preparation involves telling PowerPoint 2002:

- the type of presentation you want to run

- whether you want it to run perpetually

- whether you want each slide to appear automatically

Setting up a presentation

Pull down the Slide Show menu and carry out step 1 below. Then carry out steps 2–5 as appropriate. Finally, perform step 6.

Click Set Up Show

Re step 5 – choosing a lower resolution is one way to improve slide show performance. Another useful technique is to tick Use hardware graphics acceleration.

2 Click a slide show type

3 Optional – specify which slides run or select a custom show

For a continually running slide show, tick Loop continuously until 'Esc' and, optimally, click Browsed at a kiosk (full screen) in step 2.

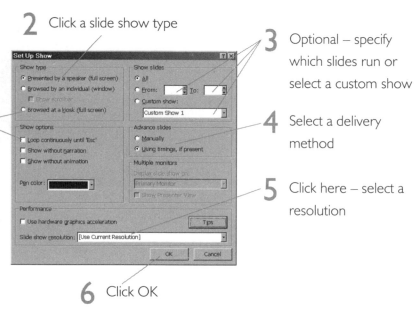

4 Select a delivery method

5 Click here – select a resolution

Re step 4 – choose Manually if you want to control slide transition, or Using timings, if present if you want transition to be in line with the timings you set on pages 170–171.

6 Click OK

Presenting slide shows

In this chapter, you'll present your slide show to a live audience. You'll discover how to move around in live presentations, and how to accentuate slide areas with the Light Pen. Next you'll save your slide show as a 'run-time' file (so it can be run on machines which don't have PowerPoint 2002 installed) and run HTML-saved presentations in Internet Explorer, another way to achieve the same goal.

Finally, you'll broadcast/view your slide show over intranets, then get information, software downloads and clips/templates directly from the web.

Covers

Chapter Ten

Running your presentation

If you have a video camera and/or microphone attached to your PC (and if you have Internet Explorer 5.1 or higher) you can broadcast slide shows live over an intranet.

Choose Slide Show, Online Broadcast, Start Live Broadcast Now. Follow the on-screen instructions – this involves:

- *specifying and saving the appropriate location/ hardware settings*
- *sending the relevant view invitations (via Outlook or another email client)*
- *running various tests*
- *starting the live broadcast*

To schedule a live broadcast, choose Slide Show, Online Broadcast, Schedule a Live Broadcast. Follow the on-screen instructions.

To view a scheduled live broadcast, double-click the broadcast URL in the emailed invitation.

By now, your presentation is ready to run. PowerPoint 2002 lets you:

1. present it to a live audience (this is the most common scenario)

2. create a special run-time file (which enables slide shows to be run on PCs which don't have PowerPoint 2002 installed) – see pages 181–182

3. publish your slide show on the World Wide Web, using Microsoft's enhanced HTML format (see page 62 for more information). This means that anyone with Internet Explorer 4 or above can run it in a way which – since the original formatting is preserved with high fidelity – is more or less identical to 1. above. So users can run your presentation without having to have PowerPoint 2002

Running standard slide shows live

Pull down the Slide Show menu and do the following:

Click View Show
(alternatively, press F5)

Carry out the additional step on the facing page.

If you allocated slide timings (using one of the techniques on pages 170-171) AND selected 'Using timings, if present' (in step 4 on page 174), PowerPoint 2002 displays the next slide automatically.

If, on the other hand, you selected Manually in step 4 on page 174, follow step 2 on the immediate right. Repeat as and when necessary.

(For details of other navigational techniques, see page 178.)

For help with any aspect of slide show broadcasting (see the facing page), see your system administrator.

If you set up your presentation appropriately (see chapter 9), step 1 on the facing page will also start a self-running or dual-monitor presentation.

By default, the mouse pointer is hidden if it isn't used for 15 seconds while running a show. To make it reappear, move the mouse.

PowerPoint 2002 launches the first slide in a special window:

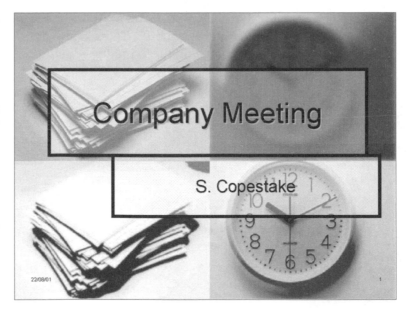

2 Left-click once to view the next slide – but see the DON'T FORGET tip

Running custom slide shows live

Pull down the Slide Show menu and click Custom Show. Now do the following:

Select a custom show

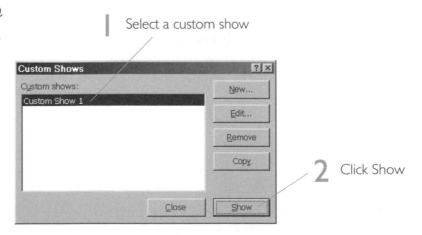

2 Click Show

Navigating through slide shows

Navigating – the keystroke approach

When you run a presentation, you're actually using a special view called Slide Show. There are special commands you can use to move around in Slide Show view. Press any of the keystrokes listed in the left column to produce the desired result (shown on the right):

Re the black/white screen commands, repeat the appropriate keystroke to return to the normal screen.

Re the 'specified slide' method – to go to slide 6 (for example), type '6' (without the quotes) then press Enter.

Keystroke	Result
Enter; Page Down; or the Spacebar	jumps to the next slide
Page Up or Backspace	jumps to the previous slide
B or full stop	launches a black screen
W or comma	launches a white screen
'Slide number' plus Enter	goes to the specified slide (see the DON'T FORGET tip)
S	stops/restarts an automatic slide show (i.e. one where the presenter is not initiating slide progression manually)
Home	jumps to the first slide
End	jumps to the last slide
Esc	ends a slide show

Navigating – the mouse approach

You can also use mouse actions:

For instance, you can use the menu to go to a slide with a given title – click Go, By Title then select a title in the sub-menu.

Action	Result
Single left-click	jumps to the next slide
Single right-click	produces a helpful menu (see the facing page)

...cont'd

You can record meeting minutes or action items during a slide show. Right-click once. In the menu, select Meeting Minder. Select the appropriate tab and complete the dialog.

Action items appear on a dedicated slide at the end of the show. To view minutes, however, pull down the Tools menu and click Meeting Minder.

If you want to run a custom slide show, follow step 1. Ignore steps 2-3 – instead, click Custom Show. In the sub-menu, select the name of the custom show.

Navigating with the Slide Navigator

You can also use a dialog route to navigate in Slide Show view.

Within Slide Show view, right-click once. In the menu which appears, do the following:

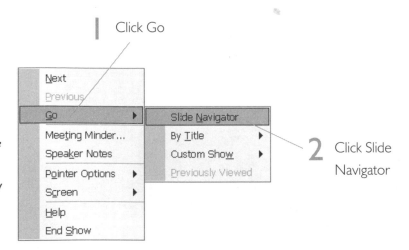

Click Go

2 Click Slide Navigator

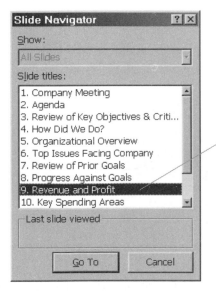

3 Double-click the slide you want to view

Emphasising slide shows

PowerPoint 2002 lets you emphasise slides during a live presentation. You do this by using a feature known as the Light Pen.

Using the Light Pen

In Slide Show view, right-click once. Do the following:

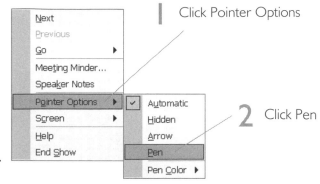

1 Click Pointer Options

2 Click Pen

Marks you make with the Light Pen are only temporary: they disappear when you move to another slide.

When the Pen is enabled, the only way to go to the next or previous slide is to use the Up or Down cursor keys.

You can specify the colour used by the Light Pen. Right-click the slide. In the menu, click Pointer Options, Pen Color. In the sub-menu, click a colour.

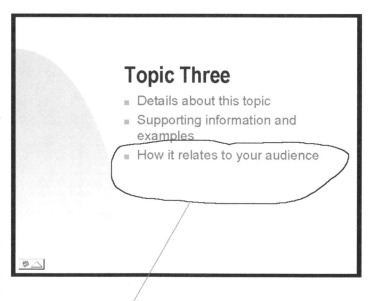

3 Place the mouse pointer (it changes to a pen) near the area you want to emphasise, then drag to accentuate it

4 Press Esc when you've finished using the Pen

Run-time presentations

If you need to take a slide show to an audience, you can have PowerPoint 2002 create a compressed – 'run-time' – file (occupying more than one floppy/external disk, if necessary) containing:

- the active presentation

- ancillary information (e.g. typeface details)

- a minimal PowerPoint 2002 viewer (a small program which enables PCs which lack PowerPoint 2002 to run presentations)

PowerPoint 2002 uses a special wizard to create run-time files.

Using the Pack and Go Wizard

In any view, pull down the File menu and click Pack and Go. Carry out the following steps:

Run-time files don't have to contain typeface data or the PowerPoint 2002 viewer: these are optional, though often desirable.

Click Next

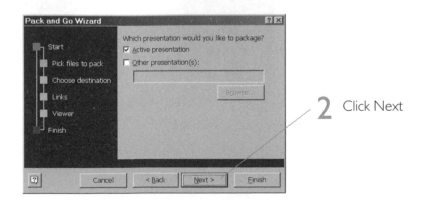

2 Click Next

Now perform the following additional steps:

Re step 5 – select Embed TrueType Fonts if your slide show uses typefaces which are unlikely to be on the destination PC. This results in a bigger file, but one which is guaranteed to run correctly.

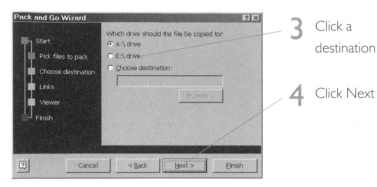

3 Click a destination

4 Click Next

To unload your run-time file on the destination PC, launch Explorer. Go to the folder containing the file. Activate PNGSETUP.EXE. Follow the on-screen instructions (when prompted, opt to run the presentation).

5 Select any (or both) of these

6 Click Next

Re step 7 – the Viewer has to be downloaded from Microsoft's web site. If you don't want to use the viewer, select Don't include the Viewer instead.

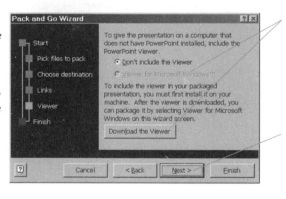

7 Click Download the Viewer then Viewer for Microsoft Windows

8 Click Next

9 In the final wizard dialog, click Finish

Assistance on the web

PowerPoint 2002 has inbuilt links to dedicated Microsoft World Wide Web pages. Provided you have a live Internet connection you can connect almost immediately to:

- helpful articles which are specific to PowerPoint 2002-related questions and topics

- a special site from which you can download useful software updates

- access to Microsoft's Design Gallery Live site (you can use this to download additional multimedia clips)

- access to further templates via Office Templates

- access to on-line services (see below)

Launching the PowerPoint 2002 web site

Pull down the Help menu and click Office on the Web

To access Microsoft's Design Gallery Live site and download multimedia clips, click Design Gallery Live:

Click Office Templates for access to additional templates.

Click Office eServices for access to on-line services (e.g. advice on storing data on the web and training).

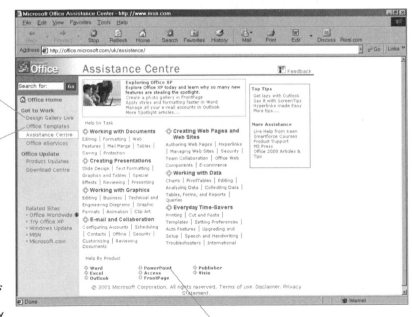

2 Click PowerPoint

3 Click an article

 You can also access a special web site which lets you download useful software updates.
In step 3, click Download Center and follow the on-screen instructions.

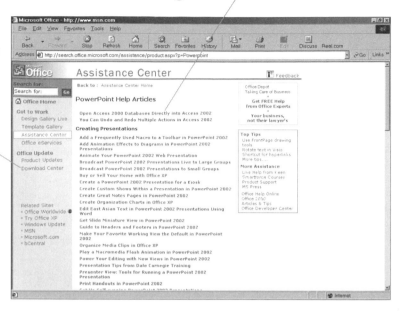

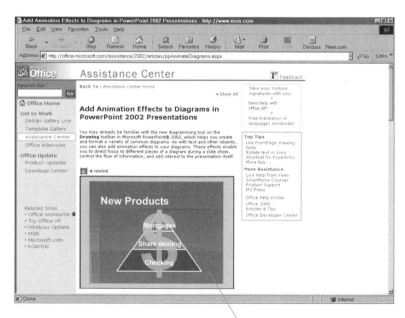

4 A helpful article launches

Running presentations in Explorer

One corollary of Microsoft's elevation of the HTML format to a status which rivals that of its own formats (see page 62) is that:

B. means that slide shows converted to HTML format and saved to the web can be run by the majority of Internet users.

A.   presentations display authentically in Internet Explorer (especially if you're using version 4 or above)

B.   you can even run presentations from within Internet Explorer

Running slide shows in Internet Explorer

First, use the relevant techniques discussed on pages 62–66 to convert an existing presentation to HTML format. Open this in Internet Explorer. Now do the following:

Here, the slide show is being displayed in Internet Explorer 5.

You can hide the slide outline, if you want. Simply click here:

Click Slide Show to run your show in Full-Screen mode

Internet Explorer now launches the first slide of your presentation so that it occupies the whole screen:

To halt the slide show before the end, press Esc.

If you allocated slide timings (using one of the techniques on pages 170–171) AND selected 'Using timings, if present' in step 4 on page 174, Internet Explorer progresses to the next slide when the relevant interval has elapsed. If, on the other hand, you selected Manually in step 4 on page 174, left-click once when you want to move on to the next slide. And so on to the end...

To close Internet Explorer, press Alt+F4.

When the last slide has been displayed, a special screen displays with the following text:

End of slide show, click to exit.

Click anywhere to return to Internet Explorer's main screen.

Index

T

U

V

W

Z